The
Police Learning Organization

A Values-Oriented, Ten-Minute Daily Best Practice for Reducing Personal Risk and Organizational Liability

Les Kachurek

NEWMAN SPRINGS PUBLISHING
320 Broad Street
Red Bank, NJ 07701

First originally published by Newman Springs Publishing 2018

ISBN 978-1-64096-283-5 (Paperback)
ISBN 978-1-64096-284-2 (Digital)

Printed in the United States of America

Dedication

This book is dedicated to Kathy, my loving wife, and Caitlin, our amazing daughter. Their love, loyalty, and boundless faith in me have not only inspired and strengthened me but also sustained me through the inevitable vicissitudes of four separate decades in policing. They make me better than I truly am, and I dearly love and cherish them.

Contents

Milestone Books

I firmly believe that most transformational leaders and change agents have many common characteristics. For example: a curiosity about the unknown, the ability to distinguish the essential from the important, the ability to communicate their vision passionately and persuasively, and the willingness to fail and the fortitude to get back up and try again. They also have an insatiable thirst for knowledge and an unwavering commitment to lifelong learning. Thus, they are voracious readers. In addition to professional periodicals, daily devotionals, and pleasure reading, on average, I read two or three books every month. Over the course of my life, that equates to well over one-thousand books. While every one of those books has added knowledge and value to my personal or professional life, some have been particularly meaningful. Therefore, whether striving to transform a traditional law enforcement organization into a law enforcement learning organization, pursuing a police chief's position, hoping to take your business to the next level, running for public office, aspiring to improve your relationships with family and friends, planning for retirement or seeking answers to vexing eternal questions, I respectfully recommend reading the following books:

- *Win: The Key Principles to Take Your Business from Ordinary to Extraordinary* by Dr. Frank I. Luntz
- *What Americans Really Want…Really: The Truth About our Hopes, Dreams, and Fears* by Dr. Frank I. Luntz
- *Words That Work: It's not What You Say, It's What People Hear* by Dr. Frank I. Luntz
- *Good to Great: Why Some Companies Make the Leap… and Others Don't* by Jim Collins

- *The 360 Degree Leader* by John C. Maxwell
- *Developing the Leader Within You* by John C. Maxwell
- *How Successful People Think* by John C. Maxwell
- *How Successful People Grow* by John C. Maxwell
- *You're in Charge—Now What?* By Thomas J. Neff & James M. Citrin
- *Emotional Intelligence* by Daniel Goleman, PhD
- *Social Intelligence* by Daniel Goleman, PhD
- *Primal Leadership: Realizing the Power of Emotional Intelligence* by Daniel Goleman, PhD
- *Emotional Intelligence Resilience* by Harvard Business Review
- *On Leadership* by Harvard Business Review
- *On Strategy* by Harvard Business Review
- *On Change* by Harvard Business Review
- *The Leadership Challenge* by Jim Kouzes and Barry Posner
- *The One Minute Manager* by Spencer Johnson, MD and Kenneth Blanchard, PhD
- *Who Moved My Cheese?* by Spencer Johnson, MD
- *Start with Why How Great Leaders Inspire Everyone to Take Action* by Simon Sinek
- *Reagan In His Own Hand: The Writings of Ronald Reagan that Reveal His Revolutionary Vision for America* by Ronald Reagan
- *The Police Manager* by Ronald G. Lynch
- *Supervision of Police Personnel* by Nathan Iannone and Marvin Iannone
- *Emotional Survival for Law Enforcement: A Guide for Officers and Their Families* by Kevin Gilmartin
- *It's Your Time* by Joel Osteen
- *You Can, You Will: 8 Undeniable Qualities of a Winner* by Joel Osteen
- *The Mind Connection: How the Thoughts You Choose Affect your Mood, Behavior, and Decisions* by Joyce Meyer
- *Right People, Right Place, Right Plan: Discerning the Voice of God* by Jentezen Franklin

- *Waiting on God: Strength for Today and Hope for Tomorrow* by Charles F. Stanley

As a career police officer, supervisor, commander, and executive, I'm proud to have served six distinctly diverse communities across four states on five different decades. I began my career in an era where most American cops, including me, carried a six-shot revolver and twelve extra bullets individually inserted in loops attached to the gun belt. During that era, very little professional development education and training was offered. In one state where I worked as a certified police officer, licensed hairdressers had more stringent annual professional development requirements than law enforcement professionals.

Like some of my colleagues of that time, I made my share of mistakes. Fortunately, my mistakes were mistakes of the head, rather than malevolent, unethical mistakes of the heart. Even so, not knowing any better offered little solace following errors that could and should have been prevented. Yes, I incurred unnecessary risks, and, yes, I was sued. Worst of all, some of my knowledge-based errors adversely impacted citizens. Indeed, I disappointed some stakeholders. Perhaps you can identify with me?

Since I wasn't receiving the professional sustenance that I needed, I became a voracious reader of cutting-edge books and professional publications. I heavily invested in myself, my career, my organization, and my community. I was committed to being the most knowledgeable member of my organization. I also made another commitment that I wrote on a piece of paper and read daily. You might call it a form of a daily declaration. "As a lifelong learner, when I ascend to a position of influence in my organization, I will work tirelessly to provide empowerment opportunities for continuous learning, growth, and improvement to all colleagues. I'll also learn from their successes and experiences."

The paper on which I wrote that declaration has yellowed, the ink has faded, and the tape affixing it to my clipboard has all but disintegrated. Yet its spirit forges on.

It's my earnest hope that you will learn from my mistakes and failures, thereby avoiding consequences of your own. Therefore, as a start, if you devote merely ten minutes every day to reading, in one year, you'll have read for nearly sixty-one hours!

Before proceeding, let me thank you for the high honor and distinct privilege of allowing me to be your learning and accountability partner.

Acknowledgments

As I travel domestically and internationally, promulgating best practices in law enforcement leadership, risk management, and strategic planning, I'm honored and privileged to build relationships and form partnerships with law enforcement leaders striving for transformational change. I'm humbled to seize these opportunities to influence and mentor these courageous, selfless professionals. I, too, have been incredibly fortunate throughout my life and during my career to have had many positive role models, mentors, and oracles. I would like to acknowledge Professor Timothy N. Veiders, the Criminal Justice Program coordinator at Niagara County Community College in Western New York. As a sophomore in my third semester at NCCC, I was an uncommitted, unmotivated student earning average grades. I took a social sciences elective course taught by a novice Professor Veiders. Tim inspired me with his erudite yet charismatic delivery, which made even the most prosaic course materials enjoyable and edifying. I immediately changed my major to Criminal Justice and pursued a career in policing. About twenty years later, while in co-command of the regional law enforcement academy on the campus of NCCC, Tim recognized my instructional talent and hired me as an adjunct instructor of Criminal Justice. His unwavering leadership, coaching, and mentoring helped me excel in the world of academia for more than ten years. Further, Tim was a credible reference for me while being vetted for both police chiefs positions I have held. Suffice to say, without Tim's influence, I would have never achieved my career goals.

I am grateful to one of my original field training officers, John Taylor. As an FTO with my inaugural police department, John not only taught me patrol tactics, communication skills, and proficiencies. He demanded values-oriented, ethical, professional behavior. John was, and remains, the most outstanding mentor I have ever known. He masterfully understood the art of persuasion and positive reinforcement. Yet, like all outstanding mentors, he also knew when chastisement was needed. He inspired and motivated me toward lifelong learning and continuous improvement. We have remained friends throughout the years. I still seek his wise counsel. Undoubtedly, without the outstanding foundation he established, I never would have ascended to the rank of chief.

I am also grateful to my best friend, the late Jay Van Orman. Categorically, Jay was the finest man I have ever known. A career probation officer, twenty-six years older than me, he taught me more about life and the true meaning of success than anyone else. Jay espoused and modeled Christian values: empathy, compassion, generosity, service, and personal accountability. If Jay ever had a bad day, no one knew it. He was the consummate optimist. He shared my triumphs and encouraged me through disappointments. Jay's authentic support, wisdom, and equanimity were unrivaled. He made me not only a better police officer, he helped me be a better husband, father, friend, and citizen. I hope the Lord sends him as my escort into heaven.

I am indebted to Dr. Grayce Lee, the president of Southwest University. Dr. Lee and the faculty and staff of SWU educated, mentored, and encouraged me while I pursued and earned a bachelor's degree and three master's degrees. While many institutions of higher education offer a variety of quality classes taught by outstanding faculty, Dr. Lee is committed to a personalized customer experience. She was never too busy for a phone call, promptly answered e-mail, and provided learned advisement. Most importantly, she understood and empathized with the challenges facing non-traditional students. The learning acquired while I was matriculated there has been applied daily throughout my supervisory, command, and executive career. My SWU education was the best investment I have ever made in myself and my career.

I offer a heartfelt thanks to the most resilient person I've ever known, my mother, Marie Kachurek. Her genuine warmth and emotional intelligence led me through some of my most significant challenges.

I thank my brother, Retired Police Captain Michael Kachurek. Every cop should have the good fortune to have served in the same law enforcement organization with a sibling for more than twenty years. He was always regarded as steady, reliable, trustworthy, judicious, and diplomatic. Actually, he was exceptional! He was truly an unsung hero in our organization.

I offer a special thanks to my former executive assistant, Kristy Webb. She is the most cheerful, energetic, selfless, caring, dedicated person I've ever known. Every police chief should have the privilege of serving with Kristy.

I offer a very special thanks to all of my police practitioner colleagues, sworn and civilian, who have shared and supported my vision for police organizations becoming learning organizations. Together, by embracing the Values-Oriented, Ten-Minute Daily Education and Training Model, we are creating the possibilities that transform our stakeholders' realities. Further, we are minimizing personal risk and organizational liability, thereby maximizing overall wellness and career satisfaction.

I offer sincere thanks to Donna Stone, the training manager at FBI-LEEDA. Donna's friendship, loyalty, and advocacy helped sustain me through a series of health-related challenges. She embodies the virtues of integrity, trust, fairness, compassion, and courage. Donna has my unconditional friendship, respect, and loyalty.

I offer earnest thanks to fellow FBI-LEEDA faculty member, Dave Allen. Like Donna, Dave's friendship, fellowship, and mentoring helped me overcome a series of obstacles. He is truly salt of the earth.

Last, but certainly not least, thanks to many of my colleagues at FBI-LEEDA and our thousands of students, all of whom I consider partners in leadership, education, and accountability.

My Personal Why Statement

The Personal Why of Les Kachurek is to spontaneously connect with others, grasp the human dimension in every interaction and situation, see what doesn't yet exist, and partner with others to bring it to life while empowering others toward innovation and transformational change that endures long after I'm gone.

Introduction

In 2013, I created the NASPA best practices award-winning Values-Oriented, Ten-Minute Daily Education and Training Model as a cost-effective, practical, and portable law enforcement education and training philosophy that can be easily tailored to the inimitable specific needs of any law enforcement organization and the nuances of any community. This model, based on six principles, has been extremely effective in reducing personal risk and organizational liability. It has achieved astoundingly positive results in both police departments I have been privileged to lead as chief of police and in many other law enforcement organizations where I have shared the model.

While not a panacea, when placed into action, law enforcement learning organizations can experience an unprecedented level of individual edification, reduced personal risk and organizational liability, improved skills, higher morale, more sound decision-making, more desirable strategic outcomes, increased citizen satisfaction, and numerous other serendipitous benefits.

Contemporary law enforcement, of course, is replete with complexity and risk. While many risk management textbooks are packed with information, they are often theoretical, written by academics, and not always well-suited for law enforcement practitioners. Conversely, this book was written by a police practitioner for the benefit of other practitioners. It is designed to be practical, easily read, easily understood, and quickly and seamlessly implemented. Containing merely six chapters, it emphasizes the necessity of continuous improvement through organization-wide learning while simplifying the critically important complex dimension of risk assessment, avoidance, and mitigation in law enforcement.

As police executives, commanders, supervisors, and trainers, we are all formal leaders and risk managers. Hence, we must seize every opportunity to educate the brave men and women protecting and serving the communities of our nation. Therefore, for these American heroes, every day must be an education or training day. The Values-Oriented, Ten-Minute Daily Education and Training Model accomplishes this. Whether implemented autonomously or as a supplemental endeavor, this best practice provides or adds, on average, thirty-two to thirty-six hours of annual in-service education. And it's virtually cost free!

Transformational change, including conversion to a law enforcement learning organization, requires outstanding leadership. Many people define leadership merely as "influence" or "persuasion." I believe that definition is too simplistic. Therefore, my definition adds "action and context." Further, in my experience, in order to be influential or persuasive, all leaders—including informal ones, must connect with their followers. These connections must be both cognitive or intellectual and affective or emotional. Connection leads to mutual trust, and the fervid synergy necessary for achieving tangible, measurable outcomes. Therefore, every chapter concludes with "connection questions." These questions allow supervisory, command, and executive leaders to continually engage, nurture, and sustain these critical connections, reinforce organizational values and identity, and become partners in learning with their nonsupervisory followers.

It is my sincere hope that if you're not already a lifelong learner, this book will inspire you on that path. As lifelong learners, we become transformational leaders. Thus, we not only imagine the possibilities that change our realities, we make a profoundly positive impact that endures for many generations.

Let's enjoy the learning!

Disclaimer

In order to breathe life into the theories espousing the manifold benefits of a law enforcement learning organization, I have chronicled real-life examples, actual conversations, and events from my law enforcement career. Thus, the information and events in this book are based on my own unbiased observations and memory. Conversations and circumstances have been reconstructed to the best of my recollection.

Out of profound respect for my former colleagues and in the interest of protecting their privacy, I have declined to specifically name the respective law enforcement organizations and precise corresponding venues. Further, I have also declined to identify any former colleague by name, rank, or title. However, generic references suitable to foster understanding of the dynamics are abundant.

Lastly, I acknowledge the axiom, "perceptions are real, even when they may be invalid." Therefore, I respectfully discourage readers from making any assumptions or inferences and drawing conclusions to any specific person currently or formerly employed in any law enforcement organization or municipality.

CHAPTER 1

Cultivating, Nurturing, and Sustaining a Law Enforcement Learning Organization

A man can seldom overcome his training.
The odds are simply too great.
—Mark Twain

These are challenging yet exciting times for the dedicated professionals across our nation, protecting and serving their communities as police or law enforcement officers. Police, as guardians of the constitutional and civil rights of all constituents, have a deep personal commitment to community policing, focusing on the safety and high quality of life expected by all constituents. Law enforcement organizations strategically plan and execute their respective mission. Mission readiness, however laudable, is simply too narrow of a focus in today's America to satisfy rapidly changing demographics and increasingly pluralistic constituencies.

During these seemingly improving yet uncertain economic and political times and with national security concerns abounding many Americans are very fearful. Therefore, they are seeking more from their government than during any recent era. As the only government organization that answers the phone and responds to anything 24 hours a day, 365 days a year, police and sheriff's departments are expected to help provide the missing pieces in their constituents' lives. This entails cultivating and sustaining mutual trust, reducing fear, including fear of crime victimization, while delivering an unbiased, personalized, and values-driven customer experience. Ultimately, police constituents not only expect, they demand their police be more accessible, inclusive, responsive, and accountable than ever.

The seminal education and training of law enforcement officers usually occurs at a police academy. There, over several months, recruit officers complete a basic training course comprising several hundred hours of academic, physical, and proficiency training. Many police academies are of the regional variety, educating and training recruit officers, representing a multitude of police and sheriff's organizations and diverse communities. Often, these academies are bound by rigid state-driven curricula designed to prepare probationary officers for entrance into a supervised Field Training and Evaluation Program. Thus, as a practical matter, their focus is not to prepare probationary officers for organization-specific and community-specific needs that frequently define success. This process begins during the supervised Field Training and Evaluation Program which broadly is designed to equip probationary officers to function as competent solo patrol officers.

Following graduation to solo patrol, too many police and sheriff's organizations stop regularly educating, training, and developing their personnel. Some cite the fiscal expense associated with in-service or external education and training. Others rely on centralized, state-driven models that mandate a designated number of annual hours, sometimes forty. These models often address high-liability topics. These include: Use of Force/Deadly Force, Firearms Proficiency, First-Aid/CPR, and Legal Updates. Other state accreditation-driven models mandate less than forty hours of annual education and training. These topical models often comprise three eight-hour blocks of instruction augmented by a firearms qualification course and, perhaps, supplemented by some case law updates and periodic training bulletins. These state-driven and accreditation-driven models, while not always aligned with best practices, meet minimum industry standards. They are preferable to having police personnel merely periodically view training videos. I actually once worked for an urban police department that had that philosophy. All sworn patrol personnel were summoned from their patrol sectors, one officer at a time. They were handed a video, instructed to watch it, and then directed to sign an attendance roster, asserting that they had completed the designated "monthly training." Most of the time, a few minutes into the video, officers were forced back onto patrol in order to respond to high-priority calls. Ultimately, irrespective of the quality of even the most professionally produced videos, they are merely audiovisual aids designed to enhance formal education and training classes. Autonomously, even the best videos are not akin to education or training. Thus, this approach is an abject failure.

Law enforcement, of course, is overflowing with potential personal risk and organizational liability. In fact, virtually every strategic and operational decision carries potential personal risk and organizational liability. Daily, police and sheriff's organizations nationwide are served with legal documents. These documents, sometimes referred to as a Notice of Claim or Tolling Agreement, are the precursor to civil litigation against a law enforcement organization, specific personnel, and the respective state or municipal venue. Receiving such notice merely communicates that civil litigation may be forthcoming, not necessarily that law enforcement personnel are guilty of any negligence, recklessness, or any wrongdoing. That, of course, is a matter for a court to decide. Whether the allegations are feckless, as many are, have merit or are debatable, receiving such notice is never desirable for the potential defendants.

All potential and actual lawsuits filed against law enforcement organizations and their agents have inimitable characteristics specific to the respective allegations. Just as no two incidents requiring police intervention are identical, no two civil claims are identical. However, during discovery motions, there are three absolutes. The plaintiff's counsel will always obtain the defendant's police academy education and training records, field training and evaluation records, and in-service education and training records. Then, they will scrutinize those records. Lastly, they will attempt to portray the education and training as inadequate, deficient, or negligent. Whether they are able to successfully denigrate those records depends largely on the quality of the education and training and the corresponding quality of the documentation and recordkeeping. Thus, knowledge is the foundation of all police activities and operations. Just as every building depends on a proper foundation to remain upright, all law enforcement organizations, in order to avoid the manifold pitfalls of a litigious society, should on a daily basis educate and train their personnel in accordance with the findings of a judicious risk assessment and ever-evolving best practices.

Think of daily education and training for law enforcement personnel as professional sustenance. Law enforcement supervisors or commanders would not send any officer on patrol or into the field without their firearm, ammunition, body armor, restraint devices, and other personal protective equipment. Yet, metaphorically, this is what occurs when law enforcement personnel are not equipped with the knowledge and proficiency necessary to maximize officer and citizen safety, provide an outstanding customer experience, and minimize personal and organizational liability by identifying and avoiding predictable risks. Hence, since every day presents myriad risks, every day should be an education or training day designed to prevent, or at the very least, mitigate identifiable risks.

Anyone who has ever been a member of any law enforcement organization knows that rank-and-file officers despise two things: change and the current state of their organization. Thus, like almost any change, transforming a law enforcement agency into a learning organization will be met with a variety of responses. It's always advisable for leaders seeking meaningful, positive change to adhere to a *few* broad tenets. *First*, communicate the reason for the proposed change and focus on positive outcomes. *Secondly*, articulate the individual and organizational benefits expected from the change. Further, whenever possible, add credibility to the proposed change by identifying similar success stories. *Third*, solicit broad participation in formulating the change. *Fourth*, incorporate suggestions and feedback into the formal proposed change. *Fifth*, implement the change incrementally. *Lastly*, honestly assess the change by comparing and contrasting with the desired outcomes. While assessing, remember, change is fluid. Thus, be open-minded and amenable to suggestions for adjustments and improvements.

I have always been tolerant of divergent perspectives and resistance to change. However, I must admit, I'm peevish about the retort, "We've always done it this way." I usually respond with a rhetorical question or two. "Did you travel to work today on horseback?" "Did you light your home with kerosene lanterns this morning?" Of course, my point is that historically, without the courage to innovate, rebuke status quo, and effectuate positive change, we would not have the modern conveniences that make life, including law enforcement, easier, safer, and more enjoyable. Moreover, while we'll discuss the vital role of organizational values at length in chapter 2, it bears mentioning that many law enforcement officers have the personal value of continuous improvement. Thus, the commitment to this value both denotes and connotes positive change.

So why does change, including transforming a law enforcement agency into a learning organization, create so much anxiety? Change naturally brings about fear of the unknown. Most police personnel will wonder how the change will individually impact them. This natural curiosity is the proverbial two-edged sword. Therefore, when orchestrating the transformation to a law enforcement learning organization, administrators should expect the following *five* general categories of reactions, and tailor their leadership efforts accordingly:

Rejection is the most common form of opposition. These people fundamentally disagree in principle, often vehemently, and are unlikely to ever genuinely get on board. Rejecters may include those who harbor iconoclastic or anti-administration attitudes, some union officials, dissidents, and those with an old-time mentality because education and training was sparse when they began policing.

Winning them over is usually futile. Therefore, after acknowledging them and accepting them, simply impose the change by exercising positional power. After all, it's still a quasi-military law enforcement organization. Thus, it's likely that rejecters will follow and carry out lawful orders. It's not that rejecters are unimportant. However, leaders must receive a reasonable return on investment for their time and persuasive efforts. These individuals usually devour their leaders' time and energy and provide very little in return. Rejecters can subsequently be offered an olive branch if circumstance allows.

Simple *disagreement* occurs when law enforcement personnel merely hold a different operational view. However, unlike rejecters, those who disagree lack the passion to invest a great deal of time and effort to thwart the conversion to a law enforcement learning organization. It doesn't mean they won't try to prevent the transformation. They may undertake easy or simple means to voice their opposition, such as signing a petition or expressing themselves on social media.

The best strategy to persuade those in disagreement is to show them respect by acknowledging their opposition and then give them three reasons to rethink it. Don't provide them less than three reasons. Such evidence is insufficient. Don't provide them more than three reasons. This can be viewed as too aggressive. Remember, law enforcement officers are fact-oriented, evidence-centered people. Thus, by providing them examples of facts and evidence, they may be compelled to revisit their own judgment. They may not be automatically converted. However, by neutralizing them, they can be won over later.

Some law enforcement personnel are *neutral.* They are found, to varying degrees, in most police, sheriff's, and corrections organizations. These individuals or groups can be just as challenging to persuade as rejecters because often they simply don't care to engage. Some are ambivalent. Others are uninterested. Neutrals frequently view their organization's executives or administration, depending on size and organizational structure, as simply there.

Since neutrals often aren't passionate about many facets of law enforcement operations, they acknowledge the quasi-military structure and are largely acquiescent. Further, they are mostly good cops. They understand the organizational mission, if not the *why.* They are usually solid, reliable performers. They handle their daily business without generating a lot of unwanted attention.

Neutrals offer administrative change agents a propitious opportunity to introduce new concepts and ideas because they don't have preconceived notions and biases. The challenge is to make them care enough to pay attention. Ultimately, the goal is to inspire and motivate neutrals to find the message and touch points that garner their attention. Then, they can be converted.

While those law enforcement personnel in *agreement* aren't a threat like rejecters, they may not be much better if they are passive, silent, or inactive. The initial challenge is to put them to work and make them genuine advocates. Law enforcement administrators want them to weigh in on behalf of the benefits of a law enforcement learning organization. By providing them the facts, they can politely correct others when they misspeak. Ideally, they become surrogates, changing hearts and minds along the way.

For those in agreement, the strongest motivations are the consequences of inaction. An "if/then" context will often motivate them to action. "If we don't implement this endeavor our officers may be vulnerable to the consequences of allegations of deliberate indifference." "If we fail to commit to this philosophy, and our organization falls prey to a Consent Decree, then we may not receive salary increases for a decade or longer."

Those law enforcement personnel committed to action passionately advocate on behalf of the benefits of a law enforcement learning organization, even when the administration isn't there. They refuse to sit idly on the sidelines, waiting to see what happens. They're out there fervidly working each and every day to ensure that a law enforcement learning organization is brought to life.

The only thing that action-oriented officers need is the affirmation of their executive, command, and supervisory leaders. Publicly acknowledging their support and loyalty will likely be a catalyst to do even more.

Informal leaders exist, to varying degrees, in all law enforcement organizations. While these individuals lack rank, formal authority, and positional power, they are often well-respected. They are frequently conspicuous and are always influential. They can be in any of the five previously described categories. Thus, when orchestrating the transformation to a law enforcement learning organization, formal leaders would be wise to identify them and make every reasonable effort to gain their comportment.

Persuasion connotes the art of change. Thus, the universal key to successful persuasion is understanding the values, beliefs, opinions, experiences, traditions, points of view, hot buttons, and countless other aspects of human nature that make us who we are. In law enforcement, add suspicions to the list of potential impediments to change. Most successful law enforcement officers are inherently suspicious. This trait can be an asset during street encounters and interrogations. However, it can be a liability to successfully introducing and implementing organizational change. Therefore, law enforcement administrators and their surrogates must suspend any belief and judgment about others and learn to truly listen to them in a way that provides insights needed to effectively communicate.

About eight weeks into my first tenure as a police chief, I introduced the idea of transforming the police department into a learning organization with the Values-Oriented, Ten-Minute Daily Education and Training Model playing an integral role. Since it was a line organization, comprising eighteen members, the command staff, including me, consisted of four supervisory officers. Further, it was a state-accredited, unionized environment with a very specific collective bargaining agreement. Therefore, after ensuring that the proposed transformation was congruent with the CBA and accreditation mandates, I introduced the concept at a command staff meeting.

First, I clearly defined a law enforcement learning organization as one "skilled at creating, acquiring, and transferring knowledge, and at modifying its behavior to reflect new knowledge and insights." This definition begins with a simple truth: new ideas are essential if learning is to take place. Sometimes, they are created de novo, through flashes of insight or creativity; at other times, they arrive from outside the organization or are communicated by knowledgeable insiders. Whatever their source, these ideas are the trigger for organizational improvement. But they cannot by themselves create a learning organization. Without accompanying changes in the way that work gets done, only the potential for improvement exists.

Law enforcement learning organizations are skilled at *five* main activities: *proactive, systematic problem solving, experimentation with new approaches, learning from their own experience and history, learning from the experiences of others, and transferring knowledge quickly and efficiently throughout the organization.* Each is accompanied by a distinctive mind-set, tool kit, and pattern of behavior. Many organizations practice these activities to some degree. However, few are consistently successful because they rely largely on happenstance and isolated examples. By creating systems and processes that support these activities and by integrating them into the fabric of daily operations, law enforcement organizations can manage their learning more effectively. These systems and processes include: recruiting and retention programs, sworn and civilian job descriptions, promotional processes, general orders, reporting systems, computer-aided dispatch, crime analysis, demographic data collection, crime prevention, community outreach, accreditation mandates, social media and technology, internal affairs paradigms, SWOT analyses, and a host of others.

Proactive, systematic problem-solving is easily linked to the community-oriented and problem-oriented policing philosophies, including the related commitment to predictive policing or intelligence-led policing.

Experimentation involves the systematic searching for and testing of new knowledge. Experimentation has obvious parallels to systematic problem-solving. However, unlike problem-solving, experimentation is usually motivated by opportunity and organizational or community growth, not by existing challenges or difficulties. Experimentation is easily interwoven into the strategic management philosophy. It is especially well-suited to the results of quarterly SWOT analyses. This is because these risk management analyses identify organizational strengths, weaknesses, opportunities, and threats. Specifically, identified strengths are accentuated, weaknesses are minimized or improved, opportunities for improvement are seized, and threats are eliminated or converted into opportunities. We will explore the process and benefits of strategic management, including the SWOT component, in chapter 3.

Learning from past experience entails honestly assessing organizational successes and failures. While this is also well-suited to the SWOT component of strategic management, it is ideally suited to operational debriefings and the corresponding after-action reports following tactical assignments and unusual occurrences.

Reviewing the "Final Report of the President's Task Force on 21st Century Policing" is an example of the *fourth* activity that learning organizations embrace, *learning from others*. This document spearheaded by the United States Department of Justice examined the operations of the Ferguson, Missouri Police Department. Thus, it comprised six pillars or recommendations for improving police/community relations. Ultimately, it promulgated identifying, analyzing, and adopting best practices, which is sometimes referred to as benchmarking. All six of the pillars will be identified in chapter 3.

Stakeholders are another fertile source of gaining an outside perspective. After all, who knows better the challenges of operating a small business than small business owners? Who knows better the challenges of being a single parent than single parents? Who knows better the quality-of-life concerns around schools than students and teachers? Who knows better than senior citizens the feeling of vulnerability to fraudulent schemes and other victimizations?

Community forums, townhall meetings, school functions, faith-based endeavors, citizens' police academies, and informal daily police/citizen contacts offer glorious opportunities for dialogue, mutual understanding, and prolific partnerships.

Transferring knowledge is the *fifth* main activity defining law enforcement learning organizations. For learning to be maximized, knowledge must spread quickly and efficiently throughout the organization. Ideas carry maximum impact when they are shared broadly rather than held in a few hands. A variety of mechanisms spur this process, including written, oral and visual reports, site visits and tours, personnel rotation programs, formal and informal mentoring, education and training programs, and standardization programs. Each has distinctive strengths and weaknesses. Each is organization specific. For example, personnel rotation programs and site visits may be best suited to larger, line-and-staff law enforcement organizations. These organizations often have a plethora of specialized personnel and multiple precinct or district stations. Conversely, line organizations, due to limited staffing and the corresponding need for greater cross-functionality, are generally well-suited to education and training programs and standardization programs.

Social media and technology, another one of the six pillars identified in the "Final Report of the President's Task Force on 21st

Century Policing," offers another contemporary mechanism for knowledge sharing, both internally and with the community.

Irrespective of the medium or combination thereof, it is important to understand that absorbing facts and concepts by reading or seeing them is one thing. However, experiencing them personally is quite another. Since it is extraordinarily difficult to become knowledgeable in a passive way, it is advisable to ensure that law enforcement personnel actively put the newly-acquired knowledge into practice under close observation, with feedback, as soon as practicable.

All police leaders and managers understand that their police organizations must measure or assess the outcomes of their strategic goals. If these outcomes can't be measured, they can't be effectively managed. Therefore, law enforcement organizations must also measure or assess learning.

Law enforcement organizational learning can usually be traced through *three* overlapping stages. The *first* step is *cognitive*. Members of the organization are exposed to new ideas, expand their knowledge, and begin to think more holistically. This type of thinking is desirable because challenges and solutions are perceived and analyzed from every angle without relying heavily on traditional framework. Thus, holistic thinking is more than a thought process. It's actually a physical, mental, and emotional experience, leading to realization, insight, and recognition. The *second* step is *behavioral*. Employees begin to internalize new insights and alter their behavior. The *third* step is *performance improvement* with changes in behavior leading to measurable improvements in results: reduced crime and nuisance offenses, better deliverables, increased citizen satisfaction, reduced on-duty motor vehicle accidents, or other tangible gains. Because cognitive and behavioral changes typically precede improvements in performance, a complete learning audit must include all three. Audits, whether internal or external, basic or comprehensive, are only as good as the action taken afterwards.

Surveys, questionnaires, and interviews are useful for this purpose. At the cognitive level, they should focus on attitudes and depth of understanding. For example, have new approaches to reducing crime and nuisance offenses through problem-oriented policing strategies been fully accepted? Surveys like this are the first step toward identifying changed attitudes and new ways of thinking.

To assess behavioral changes, surveys and questionnaires must be supplemented by direct close observation and feedback. Here, the proof is in the doing, and there is no substitute for seeing and hearing law enforcement personnel in action.

Finally, a viable learning audit also measures performance. Performance measures are essential for ensuring that cognitive and behavioral changes have actually produced results.

Effective performance measurements include: crime statistics, demographic data collection, performance evaluation reports, early warning systems, including personnel complaints—especially sustained complaints, employee grievances, and of course, periodic SWOT analyses.

Ultimately, any law enforcement organization desiring to be transformed into a learning organization can begin by taking a *few* basic steps.

The *first* step is to develop a *singular organizational identity based on shared core values*. This heartfelt, principle-centered concept is the organizational *why* and is the uncompromising heart of the transformation. It is the foundation of all desired learning and will be explained in great detail in chapter 2.

The *second* step is to *foster an environment that is conducive to learning*. This entails prioritizing time for reflection and analysis, to think about strategic plans, dissect stakeholder needs, assess current processes, and research best practices. Learning is unnatural when law enforcement personnel are harried or rushed; it tends to be diminished by the demands of the moment. Only if top leadership explicitly frees up followers' time for this purpose does learning occur continually. That time will be optimally productive if law enforcement personnel possess the skills to use it wisely. Education in all dimensions of leadership and soft skills is a non-negotiable. Soft skills are the foundation of all human interaction. Thus, they are also the greatest liability reduction skills. These include: escalation reduction techniques, logic, reason, patience, tolerance, empathy, active listening skills, negotiation techniques, compassion, influence and persuasion, respect for human dignity, and problem-solving abilities.

Another powerful lever is to *diminish boundaries and stimulate the exchange of ideas.* Boundaries impede coveted holistic thinking or multidimensional, interdependent, interconnected, visions; inhibit the flow of information; and keep individuals and groups isolated and reinforce preconceptions. Boundaries can be diminished with conferences, meetings, and project teams, which either cross organizational levels or by the synergy developed through relationships and partnerships between law enforcement personnel and stakeholders or constituents. This ensures a fresh flow of ideas and the chance to consider diverse perspectives. The decentralization of authority, to the fullest extent practicable, has long been inherent in successfully executing the community-oriented policing or community-based government philosophy. Thus, "boundarylessness" is a cornerstone of the law enforcement learning organization's strategy for the twenty-first century.

Once law enforcement leaders have established a more supportive open environment, they can create learning forums. These programs or events are correlated to the organization's strategic objectives and goals and are designed with explicit learning outcomes in mind. In law enforcement learning organizations, these usually take *one or a combination* of *three* forms: *strategic reviews* examine the changing law enforcement environment, community perceptions and attitudes, and social media and technology trends; *organizational positioning* consists of systems audits, which review the effectiveness and efficiency of large, cross-functional processes and delivery systems, such as reporting and records storage and dissemination, and body camera audio/video storage and retrieval; *internal benchmarking* reports identify and compare and contrast best practices and acceptable practices within the organization, with the goals of reducing liability and controlling sunken costs. Denotatively, sunken costs are those which are never recovered. While all funds spent on operational and capital expenditures are gone forever, sunken costs related to liability have an additional dubious, connotative meaning. Specifically, the dollars were wasted and the waste was preventable. Common examples include: attorney's fees, expert witness fees, compensatory and punitive damage awards, and court costs incurred during civil lawsuits.

Collectively, these efforts help to eliminate or minimize barriers that impede learning and begin to prioritize learning on the organizational agenda. They also suggest a shift in focus, making continuous personal and organizational improvement and continuous learning mutually inclusive. Combined with a better understanding of the meaning, management, and measurement of learning, this shift provides a solid foundation for building, nurturing, and sustaining law enforcement learning organizations.

Police personnel, by virtue of their nature, education, training, and experience, are some of the most alert people on the planet. They have keen observation skills. Many are outcome-oriented. For example, they don't view criminal investigations as complete or successful based on arrests. They seek justice through convictions or suitable plea agreements. Thus, formal leaders are encouraged to seize opportunities to reinforce and model successful learning-based outcomes.

During my first tenure as a police chief, my staff regularly demonstrated values-oriented, learning-based performance outcomes. I never missed an opportunity to personally recognize their efforts. More importantly, I lauded them in writing, organization-wide, emphasizing the values displayed and the corresponding Ten-Minute Education or training module.

One success I'd like to share involved a call for service concerning a young man allegedly displaying aggressive behaviors, possibly an emotionally disturbed person and maybe under the influence of some behavioral-altering substance. Several people in this public place remained there to observe the actions of the responding officers. I monitored the radio transmissions of this call and was elated to learn that it was quickly resolved without any application of force and without any criticism from bystanders. Later that day, one of the responding officers approached me. The officer informed me that due to a Ten-Minute module on Disability Awareness, he immediately recognized and subsequently confirmed that the subject's behavior resulted from the neurological disorder of Tourette syndrome. The alarming behaviors that prompted calls for police intervention were motor tics, jerking of an arm and leg, and vocal tics—loud grunting and moaning. Thus, the officers assuaged the individual and allowed him to maintain his dignity by inconspicuously escorting him out of the area and subsequently arranging medical triage for his disability. The officer further opined that if he had not been properly educated across the disability spectrum, the incident "may have had an ugly ending."

The potential consequences of an improper response and resolution to that incident were unlimited: avoidable injuries, unnecessarily traumatizing a stakeholder, allegations of unconstitutional policing and deprivation of civil rights, civil litigation, loss of credibility and public trust, poor publicity, public demonstrations on behalf of persons with disabilities, and external intervention from federal or state authorities. I encourage readers to conduct a web-based search of interactions between police and persons with disabilities. Such a search will undoubtedly unearth education and training needs.

Another event I'd like to share entailed a common, seemingly innocuous call for service, unlocking a motor vehicle for a citizen who had locked his keys in the vehicle. A supervisory officer responded and received authorization from the owner to unlock the vehicle. While doing so, the supervisory officer observed what reasonably appeared to be a small amount of marijuana and other drug paraphernalia inside of the vehicle in plain sight on the console. The supervisory officer began questioning the citizen who, allegedly, confirmed that the substance was marijuana and that he owned it and the paraphernalia. Upon unlocking the vehicle, the supervisory officer was overwhelmed by the odor of marijuana. The supervisory officer informed the citizen that based on his high level of comportment, he was going to seize and destroy the contraband. However, he was not going to charge the citizen with the respective violations of statutory law. The citizen allegedly thanked the supervisory officer who followed proper procedures for documentation and destruction.

The following day, the citizen contacted me by e-mail, with a complaint about the supervisory officer's behavior. Specifically, he alleged that the supervisory officer was rude, used profanity, and illegally searched and seized his property. Intending to discuss the matter with the supervisory officer, I found him in the communications area. The complainant was also there, conversing with a civilian employee, requesting a meeting with me. After the complainant departed, the supervisory officer, who overheard the complainant's allegations, became upset. He exclaimed that every time people get a break, they turn around and file false complaints. He added that he was tired of this and was going to teach the complainant a lesson. Specifically, he was going to retrieve the remnants of the destroyed contraband and pursue the appropriate charges.

Since the supervisory officer's words were in the presence of a civilian employee and two sworn, nonsupervisory officers, I quickly intervened. While attempting to mollify him and diplomatically persuade him to accompany me to a private setting, one of the non-supervisory officers also intervened. Using outstanding soft skills, the nonsupervisory officer stated, "I'm not trying to tell you what to do, boss, but couldn't arresting him be considered retaliation for his free speech? I remember that from the Ten-Minute module on Constitutional Policing. Again, with all due respect, that other Ten-Minute module, I can't remember the name, [Dynamic Resistance Response Model] said we're supposed to try to prevent excessive force and constitutional violations regardless of rank. I hope you're not offended. I just don't want to see you jacked-up, that's all."

The interaction between the supervisory and nonsupervisory officer was a classic example of sworn colleagues becoming partners in learning and accountability. Further, it accentuated the value of informal leadership.

I contacted the complainant. After establishing dialogue and trust, to his credit, he admitted that the supervisory officer had not behaved inappropriately. Thus, he declined to file a formal personnel complaint.

I had a verbal counseling session with the supervisory officer, in which I thanked him for his leadership. After all, he was one of those responsible for developing the informal leadership within the organization. We then spoke about our organizational identity and core values and discussed ways in which we could emphasize these to maximize learning from this incident. We further agreed that moving forward, we would place an even greater emphasis on our organizational identity and core values, the significance of which will be explored in great depth in chapter 2.

I could have written about numerous incidents where sworn members of my staff converted knowledge gleaned from Values-Oriented, Ten-Minute modules into desirable action, avoiding or mitigating risk, and delivering diverse stakeholders an outstanding customer experience. I chose those two incidents because if the intervention had been untimely or improper, one or both could have ended with allegations of unconstitutional policing. This is significant because allegations of unconstitutional policing is one of the most significant potential sources of criminal and civil liability facing American law enforcement organizations and their personnel. Fortunately, as an identifiable, predictable risk, it's also an avoidable risk. In chapter 3, we'll explore the concept of unconstitutional policing, examine associated risks, and strategize holistic learning-based methods for avoiding this threat.

In the interest of full disclosure and complete transparency, I've chosen to share another incident where preliminarily, it appeared that a four-part, Ten-Minute module failed; but ultimately, helped salvage the career of a nonsupervisory officer.

I personally received a complaint of alleged misconduct by a young nonsupervisory officer. The complainant was a well-known, well-respected state employee outside of the police department. He articulated the complaint on behalf of constituents under his supervision. The third-party complainant asserted that the actual complainants reported to him that one of their roommates was involved in a consensual intimate relationship with the nonsupervisory officer. The complainants and their roommate were residing in a state-owned dwelling. Thus, while all residents had a proprietary interest in the dwelling, they also had obligations and behavioral restrictions, delineated in a written code of conduct similar to a lease. Essentially, the complainants contended that frequently, while off-duty, the nonsupervisory officer was present in their dwelling. They further asserted that while there, he had allegedly been interfering with the official employment-related duties of one of the roommates, also a state employee. Moreover, he was alleged to have lodged there overnight on more than one occasion. While lodging overnight and allegedly engaging in mutually consensual exchanges of affection, the nonsupervisory officer and respective roommate were alleged to have disrupted the quiescence and quality of life of the other roommates. Ultimately, since the dwelling was a hybrid environment, simultaneously a residence and workplace, the complaint was purported to be under the dimension of allegedly creating a hostile work environment.

Hostile work environment allegations are viewed as especially pernicious because they often connote sexual harassment and discrimination even when voiced by a third-party, who was not an intended target. For example, consider the recent barrage of complaints levied at US Congressional members. Even when sexual harassment is not alleged, hostile environment claims always involve unwanted, unnecessary behaviors that are persistent and pervasive and unrelated to organizational processes and desired outcomes.

I was particularly disheartened by these allegations because the investigation revealed that the nonsupervisory officer had lodged overnight as alleged while completing the Values-Oriented, Ten-minute modules on "Police Ethics." Further, he had also recently completed the modules on "Sexual Harassment Prevention," which included third-party harassment. In-service records indicated that he had met the comprehension check of all learning objectives. This had been affirmed in writing by a supervisory officer.

During the investigation, I learned that prior to engaging in the alleged behavior, the nonsupervisory officer consulted a supervisory officer. The nonsupervisory officer, a linear thinker, inquired about the presence of any organizational directive specifically prohibiting an intimate relationship and lodging overnight in a state-owned dwelling. The supervisory officer was a decent person and a quality supervisor. However, also a classic black-and-white linear thinker, he replied, "No, nothing that specific." Thus, the supervisory officer failed to recognize the provision in a general order that prohibited all personnel from "engaging in any behavior that, if made public, may result in a loss of individual credibility; or that may bring the organization into disrepute; and may result in a loss of public trust."

I was present during the internal inquiry when the nonsupervisory officer stipulated, perceptions aside, that he had engaged in some of the alleged behaviors. I felt his angst as he was repeatedly shown evidence of having completed the aforementioned Ten-Minute modules. The evidence included rosters, learning objectives, his affirmation of having met comprehension checks, and subsequent supervisory reaffirmations. During this interview, the nonsupervisory officer revealed that the contents of the Ten-Minute modules left him "conflicted." Specifically, he had difficulty distinguishing between the spirit of the law and the letter of the law. Thus, seeking guidance, he consulted a supervisory officer.

Clearly, in this instance, the Ten-Minute modules didn't prevent undesirable behavior. However, several positive outcomes emerged: the irrefutable documentation left little doubt that the nonsupervisory officer had been properly educated and equipped with the cognitive and contextual knowledge to make the proper decision, which he failed to do; the documentation, in part, motivated the nonsupervisory officer to eschew a formal hearing in the presence of an administrative law judge, in lieu of accepting personal responsibility and holistic redress; the need for increased critical, holistic thinking skills was apparent, as was the need for better supervisory leadership and decision-making; the need to balance greater specificity while maintaining individual discretion within general orders was obvious; and most personnel agreed that an even greater emphasis should be placed on our organizational *why* and core values, which will be explored in great depth in chapter 2.

As a resolute lifelong learner, I have learned so much over the years from my supervisory leaders, peers, and subordinates, including the first-line supervisory officer in this incident. As a classic linear thinker, he viewed the world in terms of absolutes: right or wrong and black and white; sometimes, neglecting to attach context. Further, he was a very direct, although not intemperate, communicator.

Seeing this as a learning opportunity, we debriefed the entire unfortunate incident. For some time, he failed to see anything improper with the nonsupervisory officer's conduct. He ascribed this, once again, to the fact that the alleged behavior had not been specifically prohibited by the general orders. To his credit, he at least acknowledged my point of view when I asked, "If you responded to a complaint of someone throwing cannon balls from a rooftop into a crowded street, what action, if any, would you take?" He replied, "Arrest for Reckless Endangerment." I pointed out that the statutory law defining and prohibiting the crime of Reckless Endangerment did not specifically prohibit throwing cannon balls from a rooftop into a crowded street. Therefore, I asked, "Where's the crime?" He replied, "It's any act creating a substantial risk of serious physical injury to another person." He then added, "Okay, I get it."

I believe that supervisory officer experienced a cognitive epiphany. Also, to his credit, his critical thinking skills and decision-making prowess measurably improved over time.

Lastly and most importantly, the nonsupervisory officer's career was salvaged. Soon after the complaint was received, I was on a conference call with four state bureaucrats above my pay grade. They universally agreed that if the allegations against the nonsupervisory were sustained, the organization would proceed to terminate the officer's employment. I was the lone dissenting voice. I expressed, with all due respect, that the officer made a correctable mistake, which did not warrant termination of employment. After significant dialogue and my best persuasive efforts, my boss deferred to my proposed holistic plan of correction, which included several remedial Values-Oriented, Ten-Minute Education modules.

I believed then, as I do now, that the credibility associated with the industry-wide best practice award bestowed on the Values-Oriented, Ten-Minute Daily Education and Training Model played an integral role in my boss relenting.

In my observation, the affected nonsupervisory officer emerged from this incident edified, wiser, and more mature. Ultimately, I believe the lessons learned made him better than ever.

Chapter 1 Connection Questions

1. Why do you think it's desirable for formal leaders in your law enforcement organization to become learning and accountability partners with their followers?
2. How do you believe holistic thinking is related to relationships, synergy, and partnerships?
3. What specific actions do you believe formal and informal leaders should take to stimulate the flow of ideas and eliminate or minimize boundaries in your law enforcement organization?

The Significance of Organizational Identity and Core Values

*Start with Why is a manifesto for a world that
can be; a world in which trust and loyalty thrive.*
—Simon Sinek

Traditionally, law enforcement organizations have been mission centered. That is, they focus on what they do. Therefore, not surprisingly, as I travel domestically and internationally on behalf of the FBI's Law Enforcement Executive Development Association teaching best practices in law enforcement leadership, I encounter an abundance of executive-level, command-level, and supervisory-level leaders able to recite their organization's mission statement. Even those who can't, understand what it is they do. Some understand their organization's vision or how they accomplish their mission. Few, however, understand why they do what they do. Even fewer actually start with and emphasize their *why*.

Simon Sinek, author of the book *Start with Why; How Great Leaders Inspire Everyone to Take Action*, asks the questions, "What is your organization's cause, purpose or belief?" and "Why should anyone care?" Sinek postulates that by starting with *why*, purpose connects to task, thereby driving performance. Further, he emphasizes that people care much more about the reasons things are done as opposed to what is actually done. Thus, by communicating from the inside out, as opposed to the outside in, meaningful processes become honorable, transparent, and legitimate. These trustworthy processes often lead to the best outcomes. Sinek cites Apple, Southwest Airlines, and Harley Davidson as examples of corporations understanding and starting with their *why*. He identifies Dr. Martin Luther King, Jr., Steve Jobs, and the Wright brothers as visionaries who thought, acted, and communicated differently. They were innovators, challenged status quo, and each embraced a revolutionary spirit. In other words, they started with *why*.

I'm sometimes challenged by law enforcement practitioners about the applicability of the *why* to law enforcement personnel and organizations. After all, police, sheriff's, probation, and corrections organizations aren't producing goods or expecting to make a financial profit. So where's the relevance?

In chapter 1, I averred that police and sheriff's departments are the only government organizations answering the phone and respond to anything, 24 hours a day, 7 days a week, 365 days a year. Thus, through leadership, relationships, and partnerships, these guardians of constitutional and civil rights connect with constituents, create synergy, and empower them to identify, and then, fill in what's missing in their lives and communities. And they do so in a manner that transcends stubborn barriers such as race, ethnicity, creed, sexual orientation, qualified disability, socioeconomic status, and negative perceptions of law enforcement.

Since law enforcement officers are the only ones in society legally empowered to overcome resistance through the application of deadly force in the performance of professional duties and respond to resistance by applying objectively reasonable physical force, I avow that law enforcement's *why* is more important than any *why* in corporate America.

Remember, most people will only have contact with law enforcement personnel when they're vulnerable, highly emotional, possibly even traumatized. These law enforcement/citizen contacts often occur when the latter or a loved one has been victimized in some fashion. Motor vehicle stops and accident investigations are other common dynamics. Thus, irrespective of the situation, the affected citizen may not remember an officer's name or a deputy's patrol car number. However, since they're concern was the most important thing in their life at that moment, they will never forget how that officer or deputy made them feel.

There's another reason the *why* is critically important to law enforcement organizations. Recruiting and retaining top-notch personnel is currently more challenging than ever before. There are a variety of reasons for these challenges: generational attitudes, less lucrative salaries and fringe benefits, streamlined and privatized pensions, negative portrayal of law enforcement by the mainstream media and social media, and a host of others. Thus, the applicant pool is historically small. Therefore, candidates seeking this career have options. They are selecting or rejecting law enforcement organizations more often than law enforcement organizations are selecting or rejecting them.

I experienced this personally as a police chief in the Greater Cincinnati/Northern Kentucky region. One of the challenges I inherited was an inordinately high rate of attrition. My staff and I interviewed approximately twenty-seven candidates for three entry-level positions. What I learned was that just as we had been very interested in the candidates' respective backgrounds, they had been researching our organization—and me. The common denominator in the three candidates hired was their understanding and alacrity for our organizational identity and *why*. Further, they all found our values-oriented, law enforcement learning organization very innovative and alluring.

The transformation from a traditional law enforcement organization to a law enforcement learning organization is a bold innovation and repudiation of status-quo. Because learning has both cognitive and emotional components, it is imperative that all law enforcement personnel, including civilian support staff, define their individual *why*. In other words, what is every member's cognitive and emotional cause, purpose, or belief? Why do they get out of bed daily? Why does their behavior matter to stakeholders or constituents? Why do they continue in law enforcement?

Many years ago, while attending the 216th Session of the FBI National Academy, I received instruction on the significance of personal mission statements. As an assignment, I subsequently completed my personal mission statement. It was a classic mission-centered experience. However, when all was said and done, my finished product was just that, a banal assertion of *what* I wanted to accomplish. In fact, while that ten-week course was quite fulfilling, that assignment left me with an emotional void. I couldn't help but wonder about the rationale. Why did we invest two classes and devote an entire critical reflective journal to this endeavor? Why wasn't there a deeper purpose or meaning?

Several years later, early in my tenure as chief of a police department in Upstate New York, I began orchestrating the transformation to a law enforcement learning organization. This comprised implementing the five-steps described in chapter 1. Following completion of those logistical tasks, the fun began, inspiring and empowering all personnel to determine their individual *why* and then partnering with all colleagues to craft and implement the organizational *why*.

During this process, I learned that most people, including most law enforcement personnel, are "how" people. How-types, according to Sinek, focus on processes and results. They are often realists, pragmatic, and tend to live in the present. They are frequently cautious, like familiarity because of comfort, and may feel uneasy with proposed change. Many are naturally linear thinkers. That is, they think chronologically. Some are tactical thinkers. Thus, they're focused on a practical means toward an end. How-types may be skeptical of things that can't be detected through the senses or that aren't tangible or prone to traditional measurement. When presented with ideas that don't seem practical or necessary, they often ask, "Why?"

Conversely, Sinek's research indicates that "why" people are visionaries. They think holistically in big, bold pastels. They have lofty ideas, tend to be eternally optimistic, and focus on the future. Why-types tend to be imaginative, creative, and innovative. Why-types tend to see what has never existed and defiantly ask, "Why not?"

I don't mean to infer that why-types are preferable or better than how-types. Truthfully, they are just different ways people naturally view and experience the world. In fact, as a why-type, I've always considered my natural lack of ability to think linearly as a personal growth area. Thus, transforming a police or sheriff's organization into a law enforcement learning organization requires synergy from a very special partnership of why-types and how-types. Advertisers have seized on this partnership. I recently saw a television advertisement for a commercially available smoking cessation product. The father of a newborn baby declared that fatherhood inspired him to finally stop smoking. The commercial astutely connected to the cognitive *why*, the intellectual realization of the potential health detriments of smoking. It also deftly connected to the emotional *why*, the unrivaled love between parent and child. The commercial ended with the mantra, "Every great *why* deserves a great how." In other words, the product is purported to be the *how* or mechanism that brings the inspiration or *why* to fruition or the vessel that leads the inspiration to the desired result. Another commercial advertisement for a well-known chain of pharmacies took consumers for a ride down memory lane. The television commercial depicted numerous innovations and advancements in wellness. These included electronically filling prescriptions, child-resistant packaging of medications, prescriptions filled in sixteen different languages, and prescriptions refilled by scan. The commercial concluded with the mantra, "The how may change over time, but our *Why* remains the same." In other words, while things such as processes and technologies change or evolve over time, the *why* is transcendent. This affirms Simon Sinek's contention that the *why* is more than a set of skills. It doesn't change because it inspires trust and excites the human spirit.

As a practical matter, understanding and starting with *why* inspires and motivates law enforcement personnel to connect cognitively and emotionally with every colleague and constituent. This is critical because every human being has a personal unique story. By connecting cognitively and emotionally to every individual, law enforcement personnel not only add to every person's story, they become a part of their story. Hence, all law enforcement personnel are afforded an empowerment opportunity for unprecedented personal and career wellness and satisfaction.

As noted in chapter 1, any law enforcement organization desiring to be transformed into a law enforcement learning organization must take the inaugural step of developing a singular organizational identity based on shared core values. It bears reiterating that this is the organizational *why* and is the uncompromising heart of the transformation. Further, it's the foundation of all desired learning and essential for developing synergy and sustaining positive permanent change.

When I became a police chief for the first time, it was the fifth different American law enforcement organization and third state in which I had served. I had been a member of a large police department in the urban Deep South, a medium-sized police department in the rural Mid-South, a small police department in an affluent community in the Northeast, and a medium-sized police department in a rustbelt region of the Northeast. While these law enforcement organizations and communities had numerous distinct differences, the organizations had *three* striking similarities: *numerous competing organizational subcultures*; *personnel looking to each other for guidance on behavior and performance*; and *a lack of core values, resulting in an unclear organizational identity*. Yes, even the small organization serving the affluent community had four distinct subcultures in its workforce of two full-time sworn supervisory officers and ten part-time officers. The two supervisory officers represented one culture. The part-time officers had three separate subcultures: those who were wealthy, and thus, policed as a hobby; those who were full-time officers with other law enforcement organizations and were working occasionally to supplement their income and enhance their retirement; and those using their part-time position as a stepping-stone to full-time law enforcement employment elsewhere. In other words, all personnel were operating from their own individual identities.

There are several definitions of *organizational culture*. I define it as *shared beliefs, attitudes, and behaviors*. They are usually based on law, education and training or lack thereof, ethical standards, rules and regulations, history, customs, community expectations, and other factors. Subcultures result from the perception of uniqueness in assignment, role, and circumstances. Subcultures can be dangerous because they are sometimes founded in a grandiose sense of superiority, self-importance, and entitlement. Further, subcultures tend to be a powerful influencer of those responsible for their manifestation. In worst cases, subcultures may marginalize or suffocate the true organizational identity. At best, this often leads to pervasive divisiveness and resentment. At worst, this may lead to toxicity in the environment, internal and external mistrust, and even corruption.

According to licensed psychologist and law enforcement consultant Dr. Kimberly A. Miller, "Organizational identity is a group of core values, character traits, beliefs, and actions that define a law enforcement organization; make it different, and perhaps, better than other law enforcement organizations." A law enforcement learning organization based on fundamental core values and understanding its *why* is an example of a healthy, unified organizational identity.

Dr. Miller posits that cultivating a singular organizational identity requires engaging all organizational personnel and answering the following four questions:

1. *Who are we as an organization?* This requires identifying the positive strengths-based things done ninety percent of the time.
2. *Who are we striving to be?* This requires identifying the positive strengths-based things done less than ninety percent of the time. These must be practiced, promoted, and reinforced.
3. *Who are we not?* This requires identifying the negative things being allowed in the environment, such as rumors, gossip, backstabbing, inconsistency, undermining, abuse of sick time, etc.
4. *What are the things we never want to become?* Common examples include corrupt, untrustworthy, self-serving, perfunctory, unnecessarily secretive, and isolated.

After answering the above questions, Dr. Miller recommends "shrinking the change." Conceptually, this is similar to the "small wins" component of the community-oriented policing and problem-solving philosophy. This concept effectuates positive change and solves problems incrementally. It recognizes that problems in communities don't occur overnight. Hence, they won't be solved overnight.

Incremental progress or small wins builds momentum and leads to more significant wins and long-term solutions. Similarly, shrinking the change entails prioritizing a few things the organization is striving to be and emphasizing them. Preshift briefings, staff meetings, training bulletins, policy amendments, signage, and of course, the Daily Ten-Minute Values-Oriented education philosophy are all viable methods. Once positive results are achieved, the process should be repeated until the list has been exhausted.

Following momentum and synergy from the efforts directed at the who-are-we-striving-to-be list, a few things from the who-are-we-not list should be selected. Those undesirable behaviors should be eliminated in the same strategic and incremental manner.

I urge law enforcement change agents to visit www.youtube.com and consult Dr. Miller's video, *Organizational Change*.

As well-educated, highly-trained, experienced law enforcement professional, I'm certain you've seized upon the *values-oriented* portion of this daily education and training model. Brian Williams, cofounder and CEO of OneSource Virtual, a consulting company striving to maximize customers' return on investment, declares, "Core values are an extremely powerful tool for every type and size of organization." Williams believes that core values benefit organizations in *three* main ways:

- *Core values are instrumental in recruiting the right people* to law enforcement learning organizations. Candidates with a certain set of values aligned with those espoused and modeled by the organization are often emotionally intelligent, innovative, loyal, and place a premium on relationships and partnerships. Remember, law enforcement learning organizations are adept at communicating and teaching. Thus, while skills can be learned, character and integrity are traits candidates either have or don't have.
- *Core values enhance formal leadership and help develop quality informal leadership.* These values help law enforcement learning organizations grow together, unite with a collective desire to make a difference, and lead to a singular and

healthy organizational identity because all personnel constantly subscribe to an unwavering set of beliefs.

- *Core values foster universal accountability and create a remedial foundation when problems arise.* The key to creating core values in any law enforcement learning organization is determining the individual *why* of all or most personnel and using those aspirational and inspirational values to construct the organizational values. This takes courage because values are meant to be lived, breathed, bled, and never compromised. Thus, if they're being created merely to frame and display on a lobby wall or tangentially referenced rhetorically as inauthentic talking points, results can be worse than not having any core values. Cops will see right through such a scheme. Eventually, the public will, too. Thus, the CEO and all executive-level, command-level, and supervisory-level leaders must become accountability stewards as "chief accountability partners of values."

Early in my tenure as a first-time police chief, I held a series of formal and informal values-oriented meetings for the purpose of cultivating organizational values that would be instilled as the guiding principles across the organizational spectrum. All sworn-supervisory, sworn, and civilian personnel were encouraged to participate. Input was obtained from all but one civilian member, who politely declined to make any suggestions.

Then, harkening back to my experience as a student at the FBI National Academy, I integrated a one-hour block of instruction on the significance of personal mission statements into an organization-wide, eight-hour in-service education session. However, I modified it to emphasize not what each employee wanted to accomplish personally and professionally but *reasons* they're inspired to action. I asked everyone to define their cause, purpose, and belief; to list three words that best describe them; and to paraphrase what they would like said about them when they are eulogized at their funeral. Essentially, I asked them to determine their *why*. Therefore, I should have called it what is was, personal *why* statements.

As the leader of the organization, I produced and shared my personal *why* statement first. In case you missed it in the beginning of the book, between the Acknowledgements and Introduction, it's as follows: *"The personal* why *of* Les Kachurek *is to spontaneously connect with others, grasp the human dimension in every interaction and situation, see what doesn't yet exist, and partner with others to bring it to life, while empowering others toward innovation and transformational change that endures long after I'm gone."*

I was pleasantly surprised at the nearly universal ebullience for this assignment. In fact, the same civilian employee who declined to participate initially was the only one who voiced opposition. Ultimately, that individual, a disagreeable as described in chapter 1, completed the assignment after being formally ordered to do so.

Fifteen working days was designated for completion and submission of all personal mission/*why* statements. Upon receipt, I must confess, I was truly blown away by the palpable aspiration! These were works of art. All I had to do was minor grammatical editing. Following editing, individual photos and signatures were attached to each respective *why* statement. This was done to maximize ownership and accountability of their own individual words and aspirations. All *why* statements were then conspicuously displayed in various areas of the stationhouse. Most often, when mistakes occurred, the only corrective action necessary was to escort the individual to where their *why* statement was displayed, and ask *three* questions: *"Did you author this?" "Did you mean it?" "Do you still mean it?"*

A series of meetings were then held for the purpose of integrating the suggested organizational core values with the personal *why* statements, culling the best ones, and creating a formal organizational *why* or core values statement. The membership agreed that I was the best writer. Therefore, I crafted the final product, which was similar, but not identical, to the one listed below:

Our Why

United in a spirit of teamwork, driven by a resolute commitment to our shared values, the dedicated professionals of the

Anywhere Police Department recognize that every sustainable relationship arises from a personal, human need. Police personnel strive to connect to stakeholders' intellectual and emotional needs, form partnerships, and create empowerment opportunities for unprecedented community safety and quality-of-life. Unyielding in this purpose, and dedicated to live by our principles, we are devoted to ensuring a paradigm-breaking customer experience, while making a positive difference toward the greater cause of the State of Anywhere.

Core Values

United in cause, purpose, and belief we, the dedicated professionals of the Anywhere Police Department, embrace, and live by the following core values:

HUMAN LIFE
We value human life and dignity as guaranteed by the U.S. Constitution.
Therefore:
We give first priority to situations that threaten life.
We use force only as a last resort.
We treat all persons with courtesy and respect.

INTEGRITY
We believe that integrity is the basis for constituent trust.
Therefore:
We are honest and truthful.
We make decisions without regard for personal benefit.
We are consistent in our beliefs and actions.
We hold ourselves to the highest professional standards of ethical and moral conduct.

LAWS and CONSTITUTION
We support the principles embodied in the U.S. Constitution.
Therefore:
We respect and protect the rights of all people.

We treat all persons fairly and without bias or prejudice.
We are knowledgeable about the law.
We respect and obey the law.

EXCELLENCE

We relentlessly strive for personal and professional excellence.

Therefore:

We are employee-focused and develop our members to their maximum potential.

We are committed to inclusion and equitable personnel practices.

We strive to be proactive, innovative, and paradigm-breaking.

We strive for continuous learning and improvement.

We recognize and reward outstanding performance.

ACCOUNTABILITY

We are personally accountable to each other and the stakeholders we serve.

Therefore:

We understand the importance of community values, expectations, and customer service.

We are socially responsible and transparent.

We manage our resources effectively and providentially.

We thoroughly and equitably investigate complaints against our employees.

We welcome critical feedback and view it as an opportunity for learning and improvement.

COMMUNITY PARTNERSHIP

We are committed to community policing as a philosophy, not merely a program or initiative.

Therefore:

We believe that community policing best enables us to bring our shared Why to life.

We welcome, embrace, and empower all of our public and private partners.

We understand that every sustainable relationship arises from a personal, human need.

We strive to be emotionally intelligent, people-centered, and mindful of the significance of both processes and outcomes.

We recognize that crime and quality-of-life issues are community-wide concerns.

We believe diversity enhances partnerships and galvanizes teamwork.

We continually and genuinely assess outcomes in relation to community expectations and strategic goals.

The aspirational learning occurring in law enforcement learning organizations forms the basis for the organizational identity. It's what distinguishes law enforcement learning organizations from traditional law enforcement organizations. This identity must embody the respective core values, as they are interrelated and interdependent. Further, core values must permeate all organizational leadership and management activities: planning, organizing, staffing, directing, coordinating, ordering, reporting, and budgeting. Moreover, the core values must be conspicuous in the behaviors of all personnel, both within the organization and the community.

During my tenure as a police chief in Upstate New York, I observed members of my staff routinely model our organizational core values and *why*. I could share many praiseworthy stories of their bravery and heroism. Law enforcement officers are expected to be brave and heroic. Daily, across America, they willingly, boldly, and courageously save lives, and sometimes, change the course of history. However, I've chosen to share the following simple act of servant leadership:

Police in Upstate New York are accustomed to the duty-related challenges associated with harsh winter weather. The region averages about 110 inches of snowfall per season. Following a 36-hour storm that blanketed our community with approximately 72 inches of lake-effect snow, police personnel were prepared for manifold challenges: electrical outages, frozen water pipes, injuries from slipping and falling, increased traffic accidents, more interpersonal disputes from being housebound, and a host of others. As always, I monitored radio transmissions. These transmissions confirmed that police personnel diligently and efficiently braved the elements in performance of their duties. I heard two nonsupervisory officers notify the dispatcher that they had self-initiated contact with a stranded motorist. The location was about 50 yards from police headquarters.

After a few minutes, I walked to a second-floor window and observed the two nonsupervisory officers assisting several motorists whose vehicles had been buried by a combination of snowfall and roadway snowplowing. In single-digit temperatures, compounded by a significant wind chill, the nonsupervisory officers patiently helped dig through snow and push multiple vehicles that had been stuck in snow. This was not in their job description and could not be compelled. As I continued watching, I recall thinking that I'm so grateful that these officers understand the *why*. They captured the essence of communicating from the inside out, inverting the traditional mission-centered paradigm. They were truly difference makers.

I returned to my desk and crafted an e-mail, recognizing the two officers for their values-oriented service, modeling our core values of integrity, excellence, and community partnership. I sent the correspondence organization-wide and placed a copy in their respective personnel files.

I later personally thanked both non-supervisory officers. One replied, "No problem, boss. It's what we do." The other stated, "It's who we are. I'd like to think a cop would help my family in that situation."

I seized every opportunity to recognize and reinforce learning converted to values-oriented action. I believe these affirmations reaffirmed our *why* and provided learning opportunities for others.

Arguably, the most significant challenge to transforming a traditional law enforcement organization into a values-oriented, law enforcement learning organization is surviving the first few tests. Inevitably, all law enforcement organizations have their busiest seasons, well-publicized incidents, and personnel who are perceived as untouchable. Exceptions for not adhering to and modeling core values cannot be made. Such exploitation of values will destroy the trust, legitimacy, and solidarity they were created to promote and protect.

I experienced such a challenge early in my second tenure as a police chief, in the Greater Cincinnati/Northern Kentucky region. That organization had quality core values in place before my appointment. However, due to a fundamental lack of understanding of their significance, lack of emphasis, and inordinately high personnel turnover, the core values had not been impactful.

While I respect and value my colleagues and partners from all six police departments where I've been privileged to serve, the majority of personnel that I inherited and hired during my tenure as chief in the Greater Cincinnati/Northern Kentucky region were unequaled in authenticity, character, integrity, loyalty, and can-do spirit.

While partnering to transform this traditional law enforcement organization into a values-oriented, law enforcement learning organization, I was met with nearly universal enthusiasm. With the exception of one disagreeable as described in chapter 1, this transformation received significant commitment. The disagreeable was initially passive and respectful in his opposition. This individual did not quarrel with the *why*, core values, and continuous learning, as long as he was exempted. Unfortunately, this individual had significant formal authority in the hierarchical structure. Since he wielded a lot of positional power, I not only expected, I needed him to be all-in all-of-the-time.

I was personally fond of this disagreeable. He was a decent person with a lovely family. Thus, I spent a great deal of time, effort, and energy attempting to get him on board and covert him to an "agreeable" as defined in chapter 1. My attempts were unsuccessful. Thus, in this challenge, my leadership failed. In fact, the more organizational personnel displayed the courage to live, breathe, and bleed our core values and *why*, the more this individual tested our collective resolve. Eventually, this passive-aggressive subterfuge became toxic.

As previously mentioned, one of the multifarious benefits associated with core values is the positive impact on recruiting and retaining the right personnel. Similarly, because core values demand adherence to foundational principles, they also mandate personal accountability. Therefore, core values are also a guiding force in retiring or removing those personnel who are unwilling or unable to live, breathe, and bleed them.

I regularly think about this disagreeable, pray for him, and sincerely wish him the best in his post law enforcement career.

Chapter Two Connection Questions

1. Why do you think the law enforcement profession, when compared and contrasted with corporate America, has been slower to start with, and embrace the *Why?*
2. What is your personal *Why* statement?
3. How do you describe the identity of your law enforcement organization?

Identifying Risk and Prioritizing Organizational and Community-Specific Education and Training Needs

Identifiable, quantifiable risks are avoidable risks. Therefore, predictable is preventable.
—Gordon Graham

Many years ago, as a young first-line police supervisor and training director, I had the good fortune to attend a professional development seminar featuring the venerable Gordon Graham as keynote speaker. On that bitter cold winter day in Upstate New York, this unpretentious, witty, brilliant pioneer of public safety risk management changed my life. Instantly, I became one of his disciples. Since that time, I've attended several other professional development conferences where he was prominently featured. Each time, I listened attentively, took copious notes, and always converted what I had learned from Graham into organization-wide learning. Further, I have often visited Gordon Graham's website, www.lexipol.com, for a wealth of resources including my favorite, Gordon's Tip of the Day video presentation.

If you've never attended one of Graham's live presentations, I urge you to do so, as he is one of the most dynamic, entertaining, and knowledgeable educators in public safety. Graham has dedicated his life to risk management, both in his thirty-three-year career as a

California Highway Patrol officer, and as a practicing attorney. In my humble opinion, he is America's foremost authority on public safety risk management.

Risk is omnipresent in life. For example, according to www.asecrelife.com, 18,000 Americans die annually from injuries occurring in the home. From minor burns to poisoning, electrical shocks to suffocations, unintentional injuries, irrespective of the magnitude, are never pleasant. Sadly, these injuries result in 21 million medical visits each year, equaling a staggering $220 billion in medical costs. This website offers practical advice for assessing and avoiding risk in the home. It lists eight main categories of accidents, multiple sub-categories of related risks, and offers nearly three-dozen suggestions for risk avoidance and accident prevention.

The United States Census Bureau estimates that more than 323 million people currently live in the United States. Thus, the 18,000 Americans dying annually from injuries related to home accidents is relatively low in comparison to the aggregate population. Undoubtedly, the majority of Americans avoiding home-related injuries have done so, whether they knew it or not, by practicing the tenets of risk management.

Definitions of risk management are plentiful and varying. My bifurcated definition includes risk assessment as "a systematic process of evaluating the actual and potential risks that may be involved in a projected or actual activity or undertaking" and risk management as "strategically identifying, forecasting, evaluating, and implementing strategies and processes to avoid or mitigate the impact of risks."

Every day, sometimes subconsciously, law enforcement personnel assess and manage their off-duty lives with the objective of avoiding risk and the corresponding consequences. Whenever sworn or civilian personnel eat healthy foods, exercise regularly, sleep properly, abstain from using tobacco products, and effectively manage their stress they are avoiding risks to their physical health and wellness. By spending their money judiciously, avoiding excessive credit card debt, and by regularly dedicating resources to savings and retirement accounts they are avoiding risks to their financial wellbeing. Thus,

I posit that a clear nexus exists between judiciousness in off-duty behavior and risks incurred or avoided while on duty.

In addition to the correlation between off-duty behaviors and risks incurred while on duty, many law enforcement personnel are mindful of assessing and managing duty-specific risks in their professional lives. Being alert, culturally adroit, tactically proficient, and of course, regularly using outstanding soft skills are simple means of avoiding or mitigating identifiable and predictable risks. Thus, risk assessment and risk management are not foreign concepts or activities to law enforcement personnel.

In law enforcement, virtually every decision and action, including indecision and inaction, involves a level of risk. When people are hired, there is a level of risk. When people are fired, there is a level of risk. When backing-up an officer or deputy, there is a level of risk. When swearing on an Affidavit of Warrant, there is a level of risk. Therefore, my goal is to simplify the breadth and depth of risk management, integrate it with the philosophies of strategic management and continuous learning, and provide workable practices to take back to the workplace so law enforcement practitioners can protect themselves, their organizations, and their sworn and civilian followers.

Gordon Graham has declared that when risk managers evaluate tragedies, they look for the respective cause. Understanding what causes tragedy enables law enforcement organizations to design control measures and develop policies to prevent tragedies from reoccurring.

When tragedies occur, people tend to focus on the immediate event that precipitated the tragedy. For example, the iceberg is blamed for sinking the Titanic, not the culmination of events that led up to that disaster.

In law enforcement, single incidents rarely lead to tragedies. Most often, it is a culmination of events. While proximate causes of tragedies are identifiable, control measures cannot be built exclusively on proximate causes. For clarity, *proximate* causes are "acts from which harmful outcomes occurred; as a natural, direct, uninterrupted consequence and without which, the harmful outcome or injury would not have occurred." Thus, *proximate* causes are *legal* causes.

Some state courts use the "*but for*" rule to determine if a particular event was the proximate cause. When courts find that a "harmful outcome or injury would not have occurred *but for* a defendant's action," proximate cause is established.

Other states use the "*substantial factor*" test in connection with proximate cause. Thus, courts consider whether a defendant's actions or inactions were a *substantial factor* in causing the harmful outcome or injury. A *substantial factor* is "one that contributes materially to the occurrence of the harmful outcome or injury." Thus, the causative effects must be in operation until the moment harm or injury occurred.

I urge you to consult with legal professionals in your respective organization or venue for clarification and court-specific applicability.

Risk management identifies related contributory causes that were essentially "problems waiting to happen," in which law enforcement officials either knew about or should have known about. Your daily and ongoing responsibility as a nonsupervisory officer, supervisory-level, command-level or executive-level leader or manager is to ask yourself, "What problems are waiting to happen?" For example: a police detective with racial or other protected status biases is a problem waiting to happen; a corrections deputy not understanding policies is a problem waiting to happen; a police officer not understanding the Fourth Amendment is a problem waiting to happen; a law enforcement commander wanting to be everyone's friend is a problem waiting to happen; a sheriff's supervisor lacking supervisory knowledge and skills is a problem waiting to happen.

Ignoring these problems will align to create a triggering event that can be followed by tragedy and, when the post-incident investigation identifies the problems waiting to happen, someone will be held accountable.

While identifying all potential problems waiting to happen may sound overwhelming, America's foremost authority on public safety risk management has collated the thousands of risks law enforcement faces every day into the following ten categories:

1. External Risks

This is the most difficult category of risk confronting law enforcement personnel and organizations and includes risks as diverse as weather, pandemics, criminal street gangs, and terrorists or train tracks through communities. Law enforcement organizations must ensure their disaster management plans are current and work with private partners to ensure the same. Remember, many multimillion-dollar industries have disaster plans grossly out of date, but in a disaster scenario, the media will hold first responders culpable for a disjointed, archaic response.

When competing for my second police chief's position, I was informed that the organization's emergency response/disaster management plan was in its infancy. Further, law enforcement personnel had received very little education and training in this critical area. In fact, other than a couple of basic tabletop exercises, the organization and community had never partnered in any large-scale mock disaster management drills. Since this was an enormous risk, it was a major priority, but not the only priority.

I mentioned in chapter 1 that it is extraordinarily difficult to become knowledgeable in a passive way. Therefore, within four months of my appointment, following entry-level education and training, all law enforcement personnel and multiple community organizations actively partnered in two large-scale mock disaster drills. Thus, they put their newly-acquired knowledge into practice under close observation. Both drills were formally debriefed. After-Action Reports were completed and the knowledge was shared. This approach, emphasizing learning and accountability partnerships, exemplifies the guiding philosophy of law enforcement learning organizations.

I'd be remiss if I didn't acknowledge the outstanding command-level officer who spearheaded the organization's emergency response/disaster management commitment. His diligence allowed other organizational and community priorities to be simultaneously addressed. Effective leaders always prioritize well. Effective risk managers also deftly prioritize. Anything less is unacceptable.

2.   Legal and Regulatory Risks

Is your law enforcement organization in full compliance with laws and regulations? You can be certain that when lawyers investigate in the aftermath of a tragedy, that they will unearth examples of noncompliance.

Is your law enforcement organization conversant with laws like the Family Medical Leave Act, Americans with Disabilities Act, and the Pregnancy Discrimination Act? One major news network recently reported that California has just become the nation's first sanctuary state. Imagine the impact to individual law enforcement organizations and their personnel, concerning immigration-related interactions. Moreover, several American cities have previously declared themselves sanctuary cities. Of course, this has already impacted local-level law enforcement personnel more than any other group of municipal employees. Few law enforcement organizations have the resources for a dedicated in-house counsel, but your municipal attorney may not be the failsafe you think. While they may be able to offer advice on rudimentary cases, they know little about complex matters such as immigration enforcement and civil rights. Be aware of specialist attorneys who will sue your organization as they know *everything* about their practice area. Therefore, it's advisable for smaller law enforcement organizations to pool resources with neighboring agencies to hire dedicated counsel for advice on legal and regulatory risks.

3.   Strategic Risks

Strategic planning is essential not only for the next year, but for the next quarter of a century. Law enforcement organizations need to address issues on the horizon like regionalization, consolidation, and privatization. Further, individual personnel need to look out for their own future. For example, one of the most significant mistakes personnel make is not contributing to a deferred compensation plan.

4.   Organizational Risks

One of the most significant problems potentially waiting to happen is law enforcement recruitment. One solution is to decentralize the recruitment process. If every officer or deputy on duty was encouraged to recruit one great or good cop, attrition would be minimized. Just imagine the impact that same officer or deputy could have if they recruited one great or good cop every six months or more.

Once recruitment challenges are solved, the background investigations strategy must be addressed: significant financial and human resources must be invested in comprehensive background investigations. Many law enforcement organizations only do criminal background checks. However, when not impeded by union regulations or civil service bureaucracy, a best practice approach is ongoing background checks, with full checks every five years, as some personnel lose their way over time.

You may want to file this one in the category of "you can't make this stuff up." Early in my second tenure as a police chief, I conducted a comprehensive organizational audit, for the purpose of identifying specific risks within the ten broad categories identified and examined in this chapter. While reviewing personnel files, I read a Pre-Employment Polygraph Questionnaire completed by a probationary police officer hired several months before my appointment as chief. The document disclosed the following candidate behaviors: more than 150 incidences of using illegal drugs, including cocaine, hashish, marijuana, and speed; more than 500 incidences of using prescription medications, including oxycodone, amphetamines, and Quaaludes; acknowledgements of using another person's prescription medications for recreational purposes; abusing the candidate's own prescription medication; purchasing illegal drugs; operating a motor vehicle while under the influence of illegal drugs; and being in the presence of others using, packaging, and selling illegal drugs.

The candidate also disclosed a history of abusing alcoholic beverages, including purchasing alcoholic beverages for minors on ten occasions, and consuming alcoholic beverages during employment hours.

The candidate further disclosed engaging in illegal gambling for a decade and intentionally issuing several bad checks.

I spoke with the individual responsible for hiring this candidate. Specifically, I asked, "Why someone with a plethora of identifiable, quantifiable, disqualifying risks was hired?" The individual replied, "He's a good guy, and one of my relatives is his Alcoholics Anonymous sponsor. So he vouched for him."

Remember, identifiable and quantifiable risks are avoidable risks. Unfortunately, this instance of negligent hiring was not avoided, even though the background investigation revealed an abundance of disqualifying information. Actually, because of disregarding the derogatory information gleaned during the background investigation, hiring this individual could have resulted in an allegation of gross negligence or recklessness. Imagine the nearly unlimited potential consequences.

Predictably, this individual, a "rejecter," as described in chapter 1, created chaos within the ranks, devoured organizational resources, and wasted the valuable time of supervisory, command, and executive-level personnel. Ultimately, his employment was terminated without incident. I felt fortunate that the outcome wasn't much worse.

Performance evaluations must be taken seriously, as they are a great risk management tool. Unfortunately, very few law enforcement organizations take them seriously. Average personnel get overrated so no one complains, but when overrating occurs, failure is inevitable.

Again, during my second tenure as a police chief, I encountered a major flaw and potential source of liability regarding performance evaluations. The system, including the corresponding education of raters, met minimum standards and acceptable practices as set forth by state accreditation. The totality of the process was valid, consistent, reliable, established, standardized, and tested. However, explicit rater biases were conspicuous. These biases and the corresponding spurious outcomes created a significant risk and were a potential source of personal and organizational liability.

In chapter 2, I alluded to a disagreeable who never truly bought in or committed to the transformation to a values-oriented, law enforcement learning organization. This was the same individual who hired the candidate disclosing the surplus of derogatory information on his pre-employment polygraph questionnaire. While in the midst of the comprehensive organizational audit, I reviewed all performance evaluation reports. The disagreeable had only been in a high-ranking position for about a year. Thus, he had only been formally evaluated once in that position.

The evaluation form had twelve categories and numerous subcategories. It had a forced-choice numerical scale: 5 = Exceptional, 4 = Above Expectations, 3 = Meets Expectations, 2 = Needs Improvement, 1 = Unsatisfactory. The form mandated a numerical self-evaluation in every category from the ratees and the actual numerical evaluation in every category from the supervisory raters. Both were also required to make narrative comments providing examples, details and comments, and suggestions for improvement. The final numerical rating was determined by adding the twelve individual numerical ratings and dividing by twelve.

The disagreeable received a rating of 4 in eleven categories and 5 in one category, equaling a final performance evaluation of 4.083 or "Above Expectations." This did not align with an objective analysis of his job performance. Further, in the narrative, he had been praised for implementing cost-savings initiatives concerning the procurement and deployment of uniforms and equipment, for authoring policies, and for implementing new initiatives. When asked to explain these praiseworthy narrative entries, the disagreeable acknowledged that the procurement change was abandoned, because actually, it was more expensive. Moreover, he conceded that he had not authored or amended any policies or implemented any new initiatives. He rationalized reaffirming the rater's affirmations as "Following orders."

I'd like to reiterate that I was personally fond of this disagreeable. I enjoyed talking with him over a cup of coffee and exercising with him. I believed then, and still do, that he was somewhat well-intentioned. Performance evaluation, however, is not about personality or likability. It's about behavior, job performance, continuous improvement, and risk avoidance. Therefore, it must be objective and accurate. Even when it's painful for the rater and ratee.

While working diligently to empower this disagreeable to substantially improve across the spectrum, I was forced to eviscerate his job description. Thus, I assigned him low-liability tasks, with the intention of gradually restoring the original duties, as he gained proficiency. Unfortunately, the necessary improvement never happened.

Upon formally evaluating him, his final rating was under 3. Thus, his overall performance = Needs Improvement. To his credit, he was respectfully engaged during the performance evaluation conference. However, because of the specificity of unacceptable behaviors and performance, including dates, times, and locations he was unable to refute any facts.

Ultimately, objective and honest performance evaluation requires courageous leadership. In fact, it's a leadership obligation. Thus, I encourage continual honest self-reflection in this vital operational area.

In many law enforcement organizations and venues, education and training is woefully inadequate. Following completion of probation, if officers or deputies decline to promote, do they ever take or pass a meaningful test? A limited number of tasks are overrepresented in tragedies, showing the need for ongoing education and training in key areas.

Law enforcement organizations are often specialized beyond their hierarchical and organizational structures. America has state and local police organizations comprising airport police departments, university police departments, hospital police departments, and some sheriff's departments emphasizing corrections management and court security. Some centralized, state-driven annual education models fail to account for the uniqueness of the compliance obligations of these "specialty" organizations. For example, on a daily basis, university police organizations deal with ramifications of the Clery Act, Title IX, and the Violence Against Women Act. Hence, law enforcement organizations relying solely or mostly on these centralized education models are vulnerable to problems waiting to happen.

I led one of these "specialty" law enforcement organizations during my second tenure as a police chief. These organizations face all of the same challenges and threats as state and municipal law enforcement organizations and a constellation of others. In accordance with statutory law, all sworn police personnel completed forty hours of annual professional development education. This was centralized at the state capital region. Further, the state regulatory body dictated the topics and courses. Individual personnel had some latitude in the selection of courses in accordance with their interests or respective assignment. However, the regulatory body didn't offer any courses related to our organization's specialty.

Very early in my second tenure, it was painfully apparent that other than one command-level officer, one civilian employee, and myself, no one possessed more than rudimentary knowledge of the complicated mandates and obligations related to our specialty. Fortunately, the Values-Oriented, Ten-Minute Daily Education and Training Model is portable. Thus, it was quickly implemented, and produced outstanding and measurable results.

5. Operational Risks

Law enforcement personnel can be taught how to do things, but they must also be taught critical thinking skills. Thus, all personnel must know and demonstrate how to manage the risks of specific tasks and incidents. Hence, at the patrol or street level, officers and deputies need a decision-making process, especially for low-frequency/high-risk events.

During my second tenure as a police chief, I introduced a command-level officer to the genius of Gordon Graham. While he and I were collaborating on a four-part Values-Oriented, Daily Ten-minute module on "Leadership and Decision-Making," the command-level officer found the following ten-step decision-making model on www.lexipol.com. We implemented this model organization-wide and were very pleased with the results.

Step 1: What's going on? This is situational awareness. Note: if human life is at stake, immediately proceed to step 8. For instance, law enforcement personnel should think: What am I being asked to do? What is the situation about? What is being communicated to me? What needs to be decided?

Understanding situational dynamics provides the foundation for good decisions. The better understanding law enforcement personnel have, the more prepared they are to make the best decision.

Step 2: Whose jurisdiction? Again, this can be simplified. Law enforcement personnel should think, Can I resolve this? Remember, jurisdiction can be more than geography. Is this an issue for the fire department? Should a supervisory officer be requested to respond? Is a specialist necessary? Should there be an outside referral?

If the situation can be resolved, proceed to step 3.

Step 3: Is there time to think? Law enforcement personnel are sometimes presented with situations in which there is little time for critical thinking. However, the majority of situations allow for thought. Recognizing that there is time to think and using that time appropriately often leads to good decisions and actions. Remember, a few minutes or even a few seconds can aid the decision-making process.

If there is time to think, proceed to steps 4, 5, 6, and 7.

Step 4: Is there relevant policy? Regularly reviewing all organizational policies is highly recommended. Policy may dictate the decision or illustrate the amount of discretion available. Policies are typically rooted in statute, best practices, and past practice. All of these are designed to lead to positive outcomes. Further, acting contrary to policy may be a catalyst for civil liability.

Policies or general orders are integral to the success of the Values-Oriented, Ten-Minute Daily Education and Training Model. Thus, integrating them into the daily modules will be explored in chapter 4.

Step 5: What is our organization's past practice? How have similar situations been handled in the past? One of the easiest ways to upset stakeholders is to contribute to the perception that they are not being treated fairly or as well as others have been in the past.

Sound operational consistency is critical. It is also one of the best approaches to avoiding liability, unwanted external scrutiny, and poor publicity.

Past practice is not perfect. Organizations stagnate when they are averse to positive change. Thus, all law enforcement personnel, as risk managers, should make suggestions in areas where past practice is lacking or can be improved.

Step 6: Am I doing the right thing for the right reasons? This is the ethical dimension. When encountering "grey area" situations not covered by policy or affording discretion, ethics should be the driving force in decision-making and actions.

Step 7: What are the consequences? Consider the available decisions. What are the consequences of the various options? Short term? Long term? Intended? Unintended? Are there consequences for not taking action? Failing to make a decision is actually making a decision *not* to make a decision or take action. Failure to make decisions and take actions when warranted, may result in allegations of deliberate indifference.

Deliberate indifference is a different type of negligence than what has typically affected law enforcement personnel and organizations. Historically, allegations of negligence have been levied for decisions and actions that have led to harmful or injurious outcomes. Thus, liability has been incurred for the actions law enforcement personnel have taken. Under deliberate indifference, allegations of negligence occur when harmful or injurious outcomes occur due to *failure* to take action when action was required. Fortunately, deliberate indifference is an avoidable risk. Simply, decisions must be made followed by appropriate actions when decisions and actions are required.

Step 8: Make the call. In consideration of policy, past practice, ethics, and consequences make the best decision possible.

Step 9: Documentation. Remember, if it wasn't documented, it never actually happened! Thus, in law enforcement, documentation is always critical. While every incident may not require a formal incident report, options like computer-aided dispatch notes can help document decisions and actions. At minimum, documentation should include what was done, why it was done, and when it was done.

Step 10: Knowledge sharing. Through decision-making in the field, law enforcement personnel often uncover new information or identify areas for improvement. Therefore, it's important to share this information. Information sharing helps individual organizations grow and improve. It may even help improve other organizations, regionally or nationwide.

6. Knowledge Risks

Law enforcement organizations must have accurate information to make decisions. Therefore, processes must be reliable. Because law enforcement learning organizations are replete with knowledge, processes, and those managing them tend to be most reliable.

7. HR Risks

Human Resource is an expensive risk management minefield for every law enforcement organization. Thus, it's advisable to confer with legal counsel or Human Resource professionals before making any employment law decisions. As a faculty member of FBI-LEEDA, I'm encouraged at the number of Human Resource professionals attending the Leadership Trilogy classes I have been privileged to co-instruct. These personnel specialists have both edified, and been edified, by the sworn law enforcement attendees. I'm confident that as learning and accountability partners, the synergy created in the classroom has translated to decreased personal risk and organizational liability at law enforcement organizations across the nation.

A mandatory review of harassment awareness and prevention policy with all employees should be part of the performance evaluation process. In the interest of predicting and preventing identifiable risks, consider attaching a questionnaire to the performance evaluation document. The questions should be of the *yes/no* variety and require ratees and raters to initial each answer. Consider the following example:

1. Have you read our organizational policy defining and strictly prohibiting all forms of sexual harassment and hostile behaviors in the workplace?
2. Do you have any questions about the policy?
3. Did you complete our organization's most recent annual mandatory, in-service education course, and supplemental Values-Oriented, Daily Ten-Minute modules on identifying and preventing all forms of sexual harassment and hostile behaviors in the workplace?
4. Since your last performance evaluation conference, have you been subjected to any sexual harassment or hostile behaviors in the workplace?
5. Since your last performance evaluation conference, have you witnessed any acts of sexual harassment or hostile behaviors in the workplace?
6. At this time, do you want to report any allegations of sexual harassment or hostile behaviors in the workplace?
7. Do you have any suggestions to improve our organization's commitment to preventing all forms of workplace harassment?

This questionnaire prevents future malevolent, illegitimate complaints by holding personnel accountable for answering "no" to all questions. Further, it affords everyone an opportunity to report behaviors inconsistent with organizational values or prohibited by policy while engaging all personnel in potentially improving policy and in-service education. Obviously, affirmative responses require supervisory action in accordance with policy and other directives, such as union contracts or a Police Officer Bill of Rights, if applicable.

Consider the cascade of allegations recently lodged against Hollywood figures and on Capitol Hill. Imagine the difference if these entities had followed the example of law enforcement learning organizations, and taken a holistic, proactive approach to this identifiable, preventable risk.

8. Technology Risks

All organizations, both public and private, face myriad risks when it comes to technology. Any law enforcement organization could be suddenly crippled by ransomware. It's inadvisable to trust a tech-savvy millennial officer to thwart technology risks. Thus, a trusted professional chief technology officer is no longer a luxury, it's a necessity. Police leaders must budget and invest in this expertise. It could be the best return on investment strategy any chief or sheriff ever experienced.

9. Financial and Reputational Risks

Anything dealing with money is replete with risk. Law enforcement budgets are filled with risk. Grant monies contain plentiful risk. Asset forfeiture funds have a surplus of risk. Solid transparent processes for all financial issues, including checks-and-balances and periodic audits are necessary for maintaining integrity and public trust.

You may recall that in chapter 1, I referenced the Final Report of the President's Task Force on 21st Century Policing and its six pillars or recommendations for improving police/community relations. Social media/technology is one of those pillars. Thus, when it comes to reputation risks, law enforcement organizations need a robust presence on social media not only to promote positive community engagement but to defend against accusations. It only takes a handful of venomous people spreading rumors about any law enforcement organization for the public to begin believing disparaging comments. Law enforcement organizations must control the social media narrative or it will be controlled by others. Remember, facts kill rumors.

During my second tenure as a police chief, I experienced one potentially incendiary reputation risk to our organization on social media. During a stretch of winter that had been unusually cold for that region, a stakeholder observed our organization's German shepherd in the backseat of the marked specially-equipped canine patrol vehicle. The canine officer had parked the vehicle in the parking lot of a restaurant where he was taking his lunch break. The Facebook posting alleged animal cruelty, asserting that the dog had been left in a freezing cold vehicle for an inordinately long time. The posting also editorialized about the hypocrisy of police enforcing laws while breaking them.

Since all members of that law enforcement learning organization understood and embraced their leadership roles and obligations as risk managers, the posting was quickly detected. Our organization responded immediately with the facts. "Canine Hans, [which was not the dog's actual name] as a cherished member of our police department, was inside of a specially-equipped, properly heated and ventilated motor vehicle for a period of time not exceeding 30 minutes. This procedure is congruent with organizational policy, in-service education and training, and industry-wide standards and practices. We appreciate the concern of this stakeholder and are pleased to clarify the matter with facts and transparency. We look forward to continuing our outstanding partnership with all stakeholders."

A few people wanted to continue the discussion on social media. As an organization, we declined. Our only response was prompt, irrefutably accurate, totally devoid of emotion, and free from umbrage and condescension. Thus, we controlled the narrative. Ultimately, the allegation never gained traction. Imagine the potential fallout from activists and animal rights associations if our organization had failed to detect the original posting, ignored it, or had not responded in a timely and appropriate manner.

10. Political Risks

Finally, scrupulously avoiding the fray of politics is strongly recommended. Formal leaders can discourage politics by seizing opportunities to reinforce and model organizational values and by ensuring a healthy, singular organizational identity. Law enforcement learning organizations can use the Values-Oriented, Ten-Minute Daily model to educate personnel on how to avoid this potentially pernicious pitfall.

I have worked for several law enforcement organizations where the police chief was appointed by the mayor. Thus, every four years, the organization would be politically divided among those desiring to keep the chief and those desiring change. Each side chose and backed a mayoral candidate. Each side, to varying degrees, pressured other personnel to support their candidate.

As a probationary officer, a first-line supervisory officer once accompanied me on vehicular patrol. I asked if I had done something wrong that warranted closer supervision? The supervisory officer informed me that he was very impressed with the quality of my work and the way in which I handled myself. Therefore, he just wanted us to get better acquainted.

Following a brief ice-breaking period, he went into the full-court press, explaining a multitude of reasons for me to oppose the current mayor and police chief. When I explained my desire to remain apolitical, he replied, "You can't do that. If you're not with us, you're against us, and you'll pay dearly for being against us. So what's it going to be?" I replied that I'd incur the risk of remaining loyal to the administration that hired me.

Luckily, my political Russian roulette worked out favorably for me. However, that supervisory officer and those sharing his ideology ostracized me for years. Thus, every tour of duty was like being a contestant on the reality show "Survivor."

Of course, the other side fervently worked to retain power. They directed on-duty personnel to surveil the mayoral headquarters and establishments hosting fundraising events on behalf of the opposing candidate. Police personnel observed there or whose vehicles were parked in the vicinity or who were rumored to be there felt the wrath of the autocratic administration possessing the power.

Surrogates wearing badges were also dispatched to the dwellings of police personnel and their relatives. They reported back to the administration who had the "wrong" political signs on their property. They also scoured the parking lots of police headquarters and nearby streets looking for the personal vehicles of any police personnel bold enough to display the opposing candidate's political bumper stickers.

While I escaped unscathed, I have seen careers destroyed, families devastated, and lives all but ruined over politics in law enforcement. Thus, police personnel choosing to play politics, do so at their own substantial risk.

I'm a proponent of *strategic management* as the guiding management philosophy in law enforcement organizations, including law enforcement learning organizations. Strategic management has various similar definitions. I define it as "the continuous process in which organizations develop and implement plans emphasizing their *why* and core values while espousing clearly-defined objectives and goals."

Before providing an overview of strategic management, I'd like to clarify that is a *management, not a leadership philosophy.* Therefore, it is designed to improve systems and processes. Conversely, leadership is concerned with influencing and persuading people to take action. Further, leadership always considers context. Thus, while management and leadership are not identical, they're also not mutually-exclusive. Hence, managers are concerned with things and efficiencies while leaders are focused on what those things mean to people. Since people bring systems and processes to life, and strategic goals to fruition, I urge law enforcement learning organizations to equip their personnel to effectively manage and lead. The Values-Oriented, Ten-Minute Daily model can play an integral role in edifying and developing managers and leaders.

Strategic management can also be easily integrated with the community-oriented policing and problem-solving or the broader community-based government philosophy. Further, it seamlessly interfaces with any predictive or intelligence-led policing model. Hence, it has broad utility.

The *four* key *elements* of the *strategic management* process include: *environmental analysis, strategy formulation, strategy implementation, and evaluation and control.*

Environmental analysis involves comparing the individual law enforcement learning organization's situation to opportunities and threats in the external environment. Factors such as the local economy; applicant pool; societal changes; community demographic fluidity; available grants; changing entry-level education; training mandates and accreditation standards; technological advances; and the totality of the political and social justice environment could all impact the environmental scan. A *strengths, weaknesses, opportunities,* and *threats* analysis must be done during this stage. Conducting a *SWOT* analysis gives leaders an accurate picture of current *internal strengths and weaknesses* relative to *external opportunities and potential threats.*

In *formulating a strategy,* leaders chart the course for the law enforcement learning organization's short-term and long-term strategic plans, including annual objectives and goals. It is a rational, decision-making process requiring coordination of a relatively small pool of holistic thinkers or *Why*-types, and linear thinkers or *how*-types, as described in chapter 2. In short, strategy formulation entails placing the forces before the final element, implementing the action.

The *implementation* element of strategic management is predominantly an administrative and action-oriented task, emphasizing efficiency. Executive-level and command-level law enforcement organizational leaders communicate the finalized strategy to supervisory-level leaders who then pass on roles and responsibilities to their sworn nonsupervisory and civilian team members. Thus, coordination among many why-types and how-types is critical. Hence, leaders with high levels of emotional intelligence, especially those adept at the dimensions of social skill and motivation are best suited for this role. Each division, unit, platoon, and employee may have a modified role in implementing a new strategy, which may require leveraging outside resources. An education and training commander may hire an external organization, for example, to implement the Fair and Impartial Policing model to prevent biased-based policing in order to reduce liability and strengthen police/stakeholder relationships.

The best leaders and managers don't just expect, they inspect. This point contributes to the purpose of the fourth element, *evaluation and control.* As law enforcement learning organizations and personnel carry out their responsibilities toward goals, supervisory-level officers assess performance. Supervisory-level officers are instrumental. As the ones closest to the operation, they are responsible for getting the job done through others. Whether or not the job was actually done in accordance with organizational strategy requires evaluation or assessment. Thus, a key component of evaluation is measurement of actual accomplishments in relation to goals.

The *control* portion of *evaluation and control* is a forward-looking activity. It focuses on taking corrective actions when periodic evaluations or assessments are not in accordance with time-specific projections without abandoning the plan or goals. In my experience, this is the most alluring benefit of strategic management in law enforcement learning organizations.

I strongly urge you to be more qualitative than quantitative in your goal-related lexicon. For example, "precipitously" reduce or "exponentially" increase may be preferable to 5%. This is because the best strategic plans undercommit and overdeliver. Further, law enforcement learning organizations resolutely committed to the community-oriented policing philosophy must have a balance between traditional and nontraditional evaluation and measurement. For example, traditional quantitative reductions in crime should interface with abstract, nontraditional measurements, such as absence of fear of crime. Remember, failing to meet goals is never desirable. Achieving or exceeding them is critical for credibility and public trust. Therefore, language and context are meaningful. Please note the following two examples of SMART Goals similar to ones implemented and met during my time as a police chief:

Objective: As a law enforcement learning organization resolutely modeling our core values, and in accordance with best practices in risk management and police operations, exponentially increase the in-service education of all police personnel.

1. **SMART GOAL:** Increase in-service education organization-wide by broadening the NASPA Best Practices, award-winning Values-Oriented, Ten-Minute Daily In-Service Education initiative, and adding role-specific education for supervisors, specialists, and civilian personnel. [**S**pecific] Topics driven by

results of quarterly SWOT analyses, recommendations in the President's Final Report on 21ˢᵗ Century Policing, contemporary trends, and best practices in accordance with industry standards. [**M**easurable] In actual hours, topics, and personnel performance evaluations. [**A**ttainable] Building on the momentum and efficiency achieved during the four-month, Values-Oriented, Ten-Minute Daily pilot program and the recent departmental reorganization. [**R**ealistic] Cost free and to be completed during paid fifteen-minute preshift briefing, as delineated in the collective bargaining agreement. [**T**imely] The increase sought is anticipated and will be formally assessed by the end of the 2018 calendar year. *The Director of In-Service Education and Training will be ultimately accountable for accomplishment of this goal. [Status: Under Way]*

Objective: As a law enforcement learning organization resolutely modeling our core values and in accordance with the organization-wide commitment to the community-oriented policing philosophy promulgated in the President's Final Report on 21ˢᵗ Century Policing, reduce the number of residential district nuisance or quality-of-life offenses.

2. **SMART GOAL:** Precipitously reduce the number of residential district nuisance or quality-of-life offenses in Zones B, C, and D by implementing a geographic-specific and shift-specific problem-oriented policing program. This goal is: [**S**pecific] Sixty Second Daily POP objectives, compliments, admonishments, and assessments. [**M**easurable] In accordance with the SARA problem-solving model, assessed by command staff quantitatively and qualitatively; [**A**ttainable] an intelligence-driven endeavor placing responsibilities and ownership on individual officers and supervisors for self-initiation and relationship building within their respective patrol areas and shifts. [**R**ealistic] Internal and external foot patrols are a propitious opportunity to gather information important to stakeholders, build trust, and alleviate fear. [**T**imely] The reduction sought is antici-

pated by the end of the third quarter of the 2018 calendar year. *The Administrative Lieutenant will be ultimately accountable for accomplishment of this goal. [Status: Under Way]*

While all personnel in law enforcement learning organizations share the responsibility for identifying, mitigating, and preventing organizational risk, first-line supervisory officers are truly every organization's best risk managers. Since they are closest to the actual operation and have the most frequent contact and conversation with nonsupervisory officers or deputies actually doing the majority of the work, they are best equipped to identify both risks and education and training needs. Thus, while all personnel are important, they are the most vital to organizational success. Therefore, I urge all executive-level and command-level leaders to invest more education and training in them than any other group. This is especially true concerning leadership development, including critical thinking skills and developing emotional intelligence. Think about it. Not only are they currently the most important personnel, but they'll be the future commanders and executives. Ultimately, every law enforcement learning organization is only as effective as its least effective first-line supervisory officer.

In the next three paragraphs, I'd like to share an e-mail that I received from a first-line supervisory learning and accountability partner forged in the New England region. In the interest of protecting this individual's privacy, I'll refer to him as "Dakota" (which is not his actual name). Let me emphasize, this isn't about me. I'm truly not worthy of such praise. It's actually about him. I believe this individual embodies the passion, insatiable thirst for knowledge, and desire to be a transformational change agent typically possessed by first-line supervisory officers in our noble profession. These all-important public servants just need to be equipped, empowered, and supported.

> Les,
>
> I had written an e-mail to you within days of meeting you at the FBI-LEEDA training in New England; I kept reading it over and over,

but it was not conveying the impact you had on me. I am not sure that this will either, however, I could not keep letting days and weeks turn into months.

I have come into contact with many people in my personal and professional life, very few have had the impact that you had on me or left me with the perception of what a leader is supposed to be. You helped me to redefine my work as a profession, you reaffirmed what I felt a leader should be and *most importantly you instilled a belief in me that even as a first-line supervisor I could make a positive and lasting impact on the people that choose to follow me.*

I realized through you that leadership is something that is ever-evolving and that I need to continue to educate myself to remain an effective leader. Thank you for doing what you do, thank you for being a real and genuine person, and last but not least, thank you for being a man of honesty, integrity, and humor.

Sincerely,
Dakota

I also urge including community stakeholders to the fullest extent possible. Their feedback is always important in determining organizational education and training needs. Both positive and negative feedback should be considered. Citizen academies, townhall forums, police/senior citizen engagements, school activities, business associations meetings and functions, and faith-based endeavors are merely a few fertile dynamics for dialogue. Whenever possible, I recommend integrating law enforcement personnel with community stakeholders in the same learning environment.

Many years ago, when I was a police lieutenant and codirector of a regional law enforcement academy, I became aware of increasing tension between some members of the underrepresented population and certain police personnel. This resulted in a sharp rise in personnel complaints, some public demonstrations, and a few activists speaking out in public forums. I studied the personnel complaints and culled two main perception-based grievances: allegations of some officers self-initiating contact and taking enforcement action based exclusively on race without any legal and probative basis and allegations of disrespectful attitudes and poor interpersonal communication skills, leaving some citizens feeling that they had been treated unfairly and their feelings marginalized.

With the approval of my organization's CEO, I developed a sixteen-hour course, Preventing Biased-Based Policing. This topical course integrated police personnel and citizens, including many of the most vociferous critics of local law enforcement. The course was designed to provide the attendees an accurate frame of reference for each other's perspective and develop relationships leading to synergy, thereby solving and preventing identified problems.

The dialogue was unfiltered yet temperate. Police personnel and citizens became learning and accountability partners and teamed-up in several group in-basket problem-solving exercises. Dialogue continued during the breaks.

In the sixty days following the class, personnel complaints declined precipitously across the spectrum, and even more substantially in the two targeted areas.

This education-based outreach was subsequently broadened to include participation from all but one law enforcement organization in the county.

Graham's ten categories of risk as previously described in this chapter provides an excellent matrix for law enforcement practitioners to identify and prioritize risks and prevent harmful or injurious outcomes through continuous learning and strategic management. Emanating from this matrix are *four specific risks* and common tort or civil actions adversely impacting law enforcement organizations and personnel: *assault, battery, and false imprisonment; allegations of unconstitutional policing; claims of inconsistent organizational practices; and accusations of inadequate internal affairs processes.*

Assault, battery, and false imprisonment is the most common tort or civil action filed against law enforcement organizations and personnel. They are almost always alleged together. This is because arrest and detention inevitably follow response to resistance or use of force. I caution you to ensure that your statutory law governing police use of deadly force does not exceed the authority granted by the US Supreme Court in the 1983 decision Garner *v.* Tennessee. Whenever a conflict exists between state and federal law, law enforcement officers must obey the more restrictive law. Further, I urge you to integrate traditional use of force continuum-reliant models with the best practice *Response to Resistance; Dynamic Resistance Response Model.* Advantages of the *DRRM* include: it provides officers more guidance in the selection of the most appropriate use of force by placing offenders into one of the four easily recognized categories of *not resistant, passively resistant, aggressively resistant, or deadly resistant;* it accurately focuses the initial use of force analysis on the resistor and better reflects the actual events that cause police/citizen confrontations; and, because of the emphasis on officer perception, it allows law enforcement officers to explain any encounter in resistance-response or action-reaction equation.

Let me be clear, I didn't create the DRRM. It was the brainchild of FBI special agents Chuck Joyner and Chad Basile. I merely amended it by taking a values-oriented approach, combining it with the tribrid warrior/guardian/servant mindset and by emphasizing de-escalation through soft skills. In 2013, I also received a NASPA best practice award for "improving the use of force continuum by integrating it with the DRRM."

I implemented this model in both law enforcement learning organizations I led as chief. I also implemented it in a municipal police organization where I had previously held a command-level position. During one incident in that municipality, an officer inadvertently struck a citizen in the head with a flashlight. This occurred in response to the citizen allegedly fervidly resisting arrest. Unfortunately, the citizen sustained a serious head injury. Naturally, the citizen filed a civil action against the law enforcement organization, several of its agents, and the municipality. Of course, the response to resistance education and training was subpoenaed.

The municipality, to its credit, refused to acquiesce to the multimillion dollar demands of the plaintiff's counsel. They hired a law firm specializing in defending such cases. Ultimately, the case was settled for a few thousand dollars and a stipulation that police personnel were not guilty of any wrongdoing. A senior partner in the law firm sent the law enforcement organization's CEO a letter that read, "Your department's response to resistance model and training is the best I've ever seen. Undoubtedly, it saved millions of dollars."

Unconstitutional policing allegations often entail assertions of sworn law enforcement personnel self-initiating contact with citizens without having a legal and probative basis. These are sometimes accompanied by claims of explicit biases as a motivating factor. First Amendment violations in retaliation for free speech or expression are also commonplace. For example, a citizen alleged that a motor vehicle was stopped without a legal basis. The motorist exercised free speech by yelling, swearing, and insulting the officer. The motorist was warned to be quiet or risk being arrested. The motorist continued the verbal diatribe. The motorist was arrested. Thus, the motorist's First Amendment rights were violated.

Fourth Amendment allegations of illegal search and seizure, and Fifth, Eight, and Fourteenth Amendment allegations related to policy and education or training that encouraged or failed to prevent unconstitutional policing are sometimes concurrent with alleged First Amendment violations.

Constitutional rights and civil rights are sometimes erroneously interchanged. While they're not the same, they are also not mutually-exclusive. Allegations of *unconstitutional policing* are sometimes accompanied by allegations of civil rights violations. *Constitutional* rights are *protections from unreasonable government interference, as delineated in the Amendments to the US Constitution.* For example, the First Amendment guarantees, among other things, freedom of speech, expression, and peaceful assembly.

Civil rights are *those rights and privileges guaranteed to individuals by virtue of their American citizenship.* This broad spectrum includes *civil liberties, due process, equal protection under the law, and freedom from discrimination.* Constitutional and civil rights interface, because *civil* rights are protected by the US Constitution and can be enforced by the courts under 42 US Code 141. Thus, alleged *constitutional* violations often lead to allegations of *civil* rights violations by the same law enforcement personnel during the same interaction.

As a preventive measure, I strongly urge implementing best practice policies mandating Constitutional Policing, Professional Citizen Encounters, and Professional Motor Vehicle Stops. Of course, these policies must be correlated to continuous in-service education and training, including integrating constitutional and civil rights awareness into other related high-liability topics, including: response to resistance/use of force, self-initiated police/citizen encounters, and search and seizure. Policies/general orders will be further explored in chapter 4.

Of course, continuous and uncompromising values-centered leadership and oversight is necessary for reinforcement of avoiding risk and consistently delivering values-oriented service.

Operational consistency in organizational practices entails *limiting inconsistent practices* while allowing for decentralization of authority necessary to execute the community-oriented policing philosophy; asking and knowing why everything is being done, including all education and training; ensuring that off-duty conduct is congruent with professional oath of office, general orders, and education and training; understanding and adhering to mandated reporting and special relationship responsibilities; adhering to the due care standard of conduct, when applicable; and having sound Memorandums of Understanding.

Inadequate internal affairs processes may make filing complaints against police personnel difficult. Further, investigations may be insufficient, biased, and not completed within timelines specified in organizational policy. Moreover, sustained dispositions may be rare; and even when investigations have been sustained, proper corrective action may have been lacking. Inadequate IA processes may sometimes lack mechanisms for tracking patterns of misconduct; may not have an Early Warning System; and may have failed to notify complainants of the respective dispositions.

Inadequate internal affairs processes, when determined to be persistent and pervasive, have been particularly ominous because of the potential to destroy public confidence and trust. Further, these allegations have often invited external scrutiny from sources like the US Department of Justice or state attorneys general.

Under best case scenario, when ignored or neglected, the above four specific risks may be a significant threat to law enforcement organizations and personnel. In worst cases, they may substantially contribute to law enforcement organizations falling prey to consent decrees.

Consent decrees are binding, formal agreements between law enforcement organizations, their venues, and the federal government. They usually occur as a result of an investigation by the US Department of Justice, in which allegations of *assault, battery, and false imprisonment, unconstitutional policing, inconsistent organizational practices, and inadequate internal affairs processes* have been deemed accurate, persistent, and pervasive. Oversight is imposed by a DOJ-appointed entity, that centralizes organizational operations. Massive changes in policy and processes inevitably occur. The average consent decree lasts more than ten years and costs millions of taxpayer dollars.

In previous chapters, I've referenced the Final Report of the President's Task Force on 21st Century Policing. It bears reiterating that this 116-page report and corresponding implementation guide resulted from the US Justice Department's comprehensive investigation into the operations of the Ferguson, Missouri Police Department. This comprehensive document identified *six pillars* for promoting effective crime reduction, building public trust, and reducing organizational and personal liability. These pillars are: Building Trust and Legitimacy, Policy and Oversight, Technology and Social Media, Community Policing and Crime Reduction, Training and Education, and Officer Wellness and Safety.

I strongly urge all law enforcement organizations to conspicuously integrate these six pillars into their strategic plans and specific goals. Further, since this book is about transforming traditional law enforcement organizations into law enforcement learning organizations, I recommend paying particular attention to the *fifth* pillar, Training and Education, including the *eight* specific topical suggestions. Law enforcement change agents can access the entire Final Report of the President's Task Force on 21st Century Policing and the implementation guide at www.cops.usdoj.gov/pdf/taskforce/taskforcefinalreport.pdf

In my experience with FBI-LEEDA, one of my learning and accountability partners, a Virginia Beach Police Department [VBPD] lieutenant, shared their strategic plan. The VBPD's "A Response to the President's Task Force Report" truly embraces both the spirit and letter of all six pillars. Frankly, it's the most comprehensive integration of the six pillars into a strategic plan that I've ever read. As my newest learning and accountability partners, I encourage you to access their entire strategic report at www.vbgov.com/police.

Lastly, with the dual objectives of identifying and preventing risk through education, law enforcement learning organizations seize opportunities to use the low-cost mechanism of omnipresent signage in their stationhouses. Through the repetition of continually viewing these messages, law enforcement personnel assimilate these important concepts and build correct habit patterns. I had the following signs strategically posted throughout the stationhouses of the two organizations I led as chief:

Our Why

Our Core Values

Have we done everything possible today to
protect our Police Department?

Have we, the formal and informal leaders of the Anywhere
Police Department, done everything possible today to prevent
deliberate indifference? [Definition of deliberate indifference]

The Law Enforcement Oath of Honor as
adopted by the IACP, in 1989

Sir Robert Peel's Nine Principles of Policing

Chapter 3 Connection Questions

1. Why do you believe equipping and empowering all per-
    sonnel to avoid personal risk and organizational liability is
    a law enforcement leadership obligation?
2. What specific risk-related problems are waiting to happen
    in your law enforcement organization?
3. How can you, in your current role, use the tenets of strate-
    gic management to identify education and training needs
    in your organization?

Integrating Core Values and Organizational Policies into the Values-Oriented, Daily Ten-Minute Education and Training Model

*Tell me and I forget; teach me and I
remember; involve me and I learn.*
—Ben Franklin

There's a moment in life when vision, steadfast commitment, and partnering pay off. For athletes, it may be the moment they cross the finish line or hoist the trophy. Some thank God. Others acknowledge teammates, coaches, and trainers. For writers, that moment comes when they type "The End." Some reflect on an inspirational figure sustaining them during their literary journey. For artists, their signature on a finished piece is that moment. Then, they likely envision their masterpiece being admired in a gallery. Even financiers have a finish line, the zero line at the end of a balance sheet signals a very satisfying moment.

Law enforcement practitioners also experience these incredibly meaningful defining moments. I'm not referring to promotions, awards and recognition, or even that first postcareer pension check. Undoubtedly, these are great, well-deserved milestones. Yet, while cultivating and nurturing learning partnerships on behalf of FBI-LEEDA, the most common of what I call "pay off" moments I hear about are deeply personal and aspirational. One veteran sergeant told me that a young sergeant he had been mentoring informed him that within their organization he was regarded as a "difference maker." A captain articulated that his most recent performance evaluation described him as "the consummate servant leader." A nonsupervisory field training officer stated that a recruit officer critiquing their organization's field training and evaluation program described her as a "life changer." This yearning to do more and do it better, applies not only to influencing their followers and improving their organizations, but also to increasing the quality of life of the stakeholders and conditions in their communities.

As change agents, I've encouraged my learning partners to determine their individual *why* and respective singular organizational identity based on shared core values, as described in chapter 2. This, of course, is a non-negotiable for developing synergy and sustaining the transformational change to a values-oriented law enforcement learning organization.

Naturally, organizational policy and strategic planning, including formal objectives and goals, must change commensurate with the transformation to a values-oriented law enforcement learning organization. *Policies*, sometimes referred to as *general orders*, are *goal-oriented guides to action*. They are statements of intent, designed to assist law enforcement personnel through challenges and situations in which the potential for individual and organizational liability is very high. Thus, policies are more flexible than rules and regulations. Therefore, policies are interpreted through the lens of whether, in the particular circumstance, law enforcement personnel acted reasonably and in a manner likely to achieve the desired outcome. This is because unlike *rules and regulations*, which are written in accordance with whether the *letter* of intent has been observed, *policies* allow for discretion as to whether their *spirit* has been honored. Thus, I recommend the following seven steps for policy formulation, implementation, and review in law enforcement learning organizations:

1. Using the ten broad categories of risk listed in chapter 3, establish policies that guide the most critical decisions

made by law enforcement personnel and conspicuously and skillfully integrate the organization's *why*, core values, and a truncated version of the ten-step decision-making model discussed in chapter 3 into each policy.

2. Ensure that all law enforcement personnel are educated and trained in the meaning and proper application of each policy; integrate policies germane to the topics in every in-service education and training class, including important policy excerpts, into each Values-Oriented, Daily Ten-Minute Education module; and link the most important aspects of policy to learning objectives and the comprehension check. This will be described in depth in chapter 5.

3. Correlate elements of the organization's strategic plan and formal objectives and goals into relevant policies.

4. Using the SWOT component of the strategic management model described in chapter 3, continually review policies to ensure that whenever possible, they are in accordance with best practices; always at least in accordance with minimum standards and acceptable practices; are responsive to community needs, societal changes, current trends, and new mandates; and issue a *policy attestation* averring that all policies not rescinded and replaced or amended conform with established standards.

5. Without delay, communicate all policy changes and amendments to all personnel and maintain meticulous records of all changes and amendments.

6. In the interest of transparency and galvanizing learning and accountability partnerships with community stakeholders, make all organizational policies available on the law enforcement learning organization's website. Of course, certain tactical or law enforcement sensitive elements of some policies should be redacted from public consumption.

7. Encourage all personnel to make suggestions for improving policy while holding everyone accountable for adherence to policy.

In law enforcement learning organizations, policies and accreditation are inextricably linked. As a state-certified police accreditation manager, I've been intimately involved in the initial or reaccreditation processes with three state accredited police departments in two different states. Thus, I've researched, written, amended, rescinded, or replaced hundreds of policies. As a state-certified accreditation assessor, I've read and analyzed thousands of policies. Therefore, accreditation, whether through the Commission on Law Enforcement Accreditation [CALEA] or at the state level in participating states, every standard requires a formal individual policy. CALEA standards reflect best practices in accordance with established industry-wide standards. While the number of standards is fluid, it's typically in the 450–480 range. Most state-level accreditation standards mandate adherence to minimum standards and acceptable practices. Again, while the number of standards is also fluid, it's typically in the 125–150 range. Moreover, state accredited law enforcement organizations are not prohibited from adhering to best practices. For example, I implemented the best practices of the Values-Oriented, Ten-Minute Daily Education and Training Model and the Dynamic Resistance Response Model of force in both state accredited law enforcement learning organizations I led as chief of police. Therefore, it's not unusual to encounter a combination of policies ascribing both best and acceptable practices in state-accredited law enforcement organizations.

Ultimately, accreditation, under either model, is a continuous journey. It requires significant commitment and considerable organizational resources. Rarely does a tour of duty pass where law enforcement personnel responsible for maintaining compliance aren't dedicating time and effort toward the process. However, accreditation is not a panacea. It's a tool. Like all tools, it has utility. It also has limitations. In my experience, in addition to fostering accountability through adherence to professional standards, both CALEA standards, found at www.calea.org and individual state-driven accreditation standards should be considered when determining the number and exact topics of organization-specific policies in law enforcement learning organizations, even in those that aren't accredited.

Writing policies can be an intimidating, daunting task for some law enforcement personnel. However, it doesn't have to be. The International Association of Chiefs of Police [IACP] offers reasonably priced individual and organizational memberships. The cost of organizational membership is based on the number of personnel but is capped at an affordable maximum annual fee. One of the main benefits of this membership, which can be explored at www.theiacp.org, is access to thousands of model policies, covering both best and acceptable practices. Thus, rather than continually reinventing the wheel, law enforcement practitioners can choose from the model policies most closely aligning with their organization's needs. The policies can then be amended to be organization-specific, reviewed, approved, disseminated, implemented, and periodically assessed.

By now, the respect and admiration I have for Gordon Graham is obvious. The first time I heard him speak he passionately espoused his conviction of "Every day must be a training day." He focused on organizational policies as the foundation of five minutes or so of daily training during preshift briefing. After unearthing training needs through a risk analysis, Graham encouraged reviewing salient sections of identified policy with on-duty personnel. He also emphasized the necessity of maintaining accurate records of what was reviewed, by whom, and the names of those in attendance. For purposes of standardization and uniformity, the same policy review must be repeated in order to ensure that personnel who had previously been off duty for any reason received the same information.

I left that seminar intrigued. However, since my employing organization was in the process of earning its seminal state accreditation, I knew that Graham's methodology, as I understood it, was unacceptable to the state where my organization was located. Concerning education and training, accreditation standards mandated the following: a formal, written course announcement; a formal, written attendance roster; a formal, written lesson plan, including clearly-defined learning objectives; a clearly-defined comprehension check; source citations; and the name and education-based credentials of the individual preparing and delivering the instruction. Hence, Graham provided the impetus for a modification of his philosophy. Thus, the

Values-Oriented, Ten-Minute Daily Education and Training Model was born.

I launched the pilot model organization-wide with an intended trial period of ninety days, followed by assessment through a learning audit, as described in chapter 1. Ten days later, a new mayor was sworn into office. He appointed a new CEO to lead the police department. The new CEO informed me that he felt the transition of power at the top of the organization, the anticipated accreditation, and a daily education model was "too much change, too soon." Thus, in accordance with accreditation guidelines, he asked me to implement twenty-one hours of annual in-service education, in periodic seven-hour blocks. Ironically, the Values-Oriented, *Ten*-Minute Daily Education and Training Model died acutely at *ten* days old.

As time passed, and the organization became more comfortable with the new direction of the latest CEO, I periodically suggested resurrecting my Graham-inspired idea. While it never gained traction in that organization, I never abandoned it. I chose to be holistic and adopt a broad view with a broad understanding. You might say that I became my own customer. Thus, I implemented the Values-Oriented, Daily Ten-Minute Education and Training Model for myself. Therefore, I invested the first ten minutes of every tour of duty in my personal edification and professional development. Since I worked about 230 days annually, this afforded me 38 more hours of annual professional development education than every other member of the organization. I remained with that organization for about ten more years until I attained my first chief's position. Ultimately, those additional 380 hours of professional development education were akin to nineteen years of accreditation-driven, organization-wide in-service education. Since I was my only customer, I understood the concept better than anyone else. Thus, as the most knowledgeable supervisory officer, I gained a tremendous competitive advantage within that organization.

I used my education-based advantage for the betterment of the organization and community, even when it produced controversial yet positive outcomes. One such outcome entailed solving a longstanding personnel-related, operational problem in the city jail.

Upon being promoted to captain, the jail operation was added to my manifold command responsibilities with an edict to "straighten it out." Thus, I immediately conducted a comprehensive SWOT analysis. This identified and prioritized the risks to be eliminated or minimized. The SWOT analysis revealed that the most significant *organizational* risk existed in the female cellblock. Prisoners in the male cellblock were supervised by either male or female police officers. Due to a nuance in state law governing our type of holding facility, female prisoners were only allowed to be supervised by female employees. Historically, our organization never had enough female officers to staff the female cellblock. Therefore, on-call civilian female employees were hired for intake, supervision, and internal transportation of female prisoners. This system was efficient and cost-effective for generations, in part, because unlike male prisoners, the organization didn't continuously house female prisoners.

At some point, some of the civilian female employees felt that they had been treated unfairly. Thus, they unionized. As a result of their contract, they gained 24/7 employment, an hourly wage higher than many police officers, exclusivity in supervision of female prisoners, and substantial overtime opportunities. Further, they were not reluctant to file improper labor practices and formal grievances. Their sudden, vast empowerment contributed to a toxic, untenable environment. In the interest of fairness and accuracy, other personnel and myriad factors also contributed to the palpable toxicity.

I'd like to emphasize that I was personally fond of the civilian female employees. Moreover, as *neutrals*, described in chapter 1, some of them put forth a reasonable effort and took a fair amount of pride in their duties. Of course, reasonable and fair was inadequate. Others, as disagreeable employees, also described in chapter 1, either through commission or omission, created or exacerbated chronic problems. I tried leading, teaching, training, coaching, mentoring, correcting, and disciplining. My efforts produced only marginally positive results. Since strategic goals weren't met, my leadership failed.

As a relatively small group of civilian employees with a unique function, I wasn't concerned about organization-wide lack of standardization and uniformity. Thus, I turned to my trusted old friend, the Values-Oriented, Ten-Minute Daily Education and Training Model. My intention was to improve performance and behavior through a cascade of continuous knowledge in concert with the *why and develop learning and accountability partners within the group.* While researching the inaugural four-module course comprising statutory correction law, statutory procedural law, federal civil rights law, and organizational policy, I had a learning epiphany. I determined that correction law had not been amended since creation of the electronic control weapon and that procedural law prohibited any civilian from possessing any electronic control weapon or stun gun. Therefore, with the approval of the organization's CEO, and the support of the venue's mayor and municipal administrator, I wrote a policy giving sworn police officers assigned to jail duty, controlled access to an electronic control weapon. This was designed to increase the safety of police personnel and prisoners. It also, some opined, effectively and serendipitously, ended the employment of the civilian females supervising female prisoners.

The SWOT analysis of the jail operations also revealed another related glaring operational inefficiency and risk. Since the female cellblock had been predominantly vacant during the B and C shifts, the civilian female employees had produced only a negligible return on the organizational investment in them. As civilians with a specific union contract, they were not cross-functional. Therefore, during prolonged periods of cellblock vacancy, they had not been producing. Conversely, by replacing them with female police officers, prisoners received better, more professional supervision. Further, during times of cellblock vacancy, female officers were transferred to patrol duties. This enhanced officer safety and reduced Patrol Division overtime costs. As I noted earlier, the transition from civilian employees to police officers in the cellblock wasn't without controversy. The police and municipal administrations were pleased with the average annual payroll savings of approximately $200,000.00. Most police officers and supervisors also applauded the change. Of course, the affected civilian employees, their families, and their union felt the decision was unfair. Interestingly, the union representing the affected employees, offered only cursory resistance to eliminating their employment.

This well-known union has a strong presence in America and a plethora of resources. However, the union's passive approach deviated from their historically aggressive defense of those employees, including allocation of resources far exceeding the corresponding local union dues. I believe that since the formal policy governing this substantial organizational change was founded in statute and best practice, as recommended in chapter 3, it was impervious to a credible attack from the union. Thus, in the separation agreement, the union stipulated to a nominal severance package. A lawsuit was never filed.

Ultimately, I stand by my decision, the corresponding action, and the collective outcome. This is because the Values-Oriented, Ten-Minute Daily Education and Training Model isn't an innovation. It is a breakthrough that shakes off conventional constraints, in lieu of bold expectations. This outcome affirmed the veracity of this model. I've since experienced numerous reaffirmations.

I'm guessing that by reading this book, you are always thinking about law enforcement and life, in strategic, unique ways. In other words, you see the entire picture. Therefore, I'm optimistic that transforming your organization into a law enforcement learning organization will result in a break-up with conventionality, a break-out from the ordinary, and a breakthrough to the extraordinary. Can you think of a better use of ten minutes?

Chapter 4 Connection Questions

1. Why have the most influential decision-makers in your law enforcement organization decided for or against pursuing accreditation?
2. What specific recommendations do you have for amending or improving the policies or general orders in your law enforcement organization?
3. How would you integrate key elements of your organization's strategic plan into the policies or general orders?

Implementing and Formatting the Values-Oriented, Daily Ten-Minute Education and Training Model

You'll turn out ordinary if you're not careful.
—Ann Brashares

As a police chief, in accordance with our organization's *why and core values* and our unwavering commitment to the community-oriented policing and problem-solving philosophy, I authored and introduced our organization's "*Contract with our Stakeholders.*" This document promulgated our law enforcement learning organization's commitment to fair, impartial policing in accordance with the US Constitution. Further, it outlined a strategy for creating accountability partners by increasing police/stakeholder interactions, including robust learning-based internship opportunities for our constituents. Moreover, in the interest of transparency, it delineated both the *why* and how of the demographic data collection provision of the contract. All police personnel read, agreed, and signed the document. It was then disseminated throughout the community for affirmation. Momentum surged as stakeholders affirmed the contract's tenets and assumed co-ownership with their signatures. Thus, the contract became a covenant. About that time, a supervisory-level officer asked, "Chief, why is it that every time we accomplish something, you want more, like this contract thing? I mean, will you ever be satisfied?" I replied, "I don't believe God created cops to be ordinary. So, while I appreciate everyone's effort and am pleased with our direction, I'll never be satisfied."

I'm guessing that you're not ordinary either. If you were, you wouldn't have answered the calling of law enforcement. At the very least, you wouldn't have made it your career. Therefore, I'm gathering that you engage, inspire, persist, and prevail. I imagine you work as long and hard as necessary to get the job done properly. I'll bet, like me, you've had your share of disappointments and failures; you accepted responsibility; learned from them; and emerged even more committed and determined.

The Values-Oriented, Ten-Minute Daily Education and Training Model was designed to be portable. Therefore, while I'll provide a matrix for implementation, no one, and certainly not me, knows the fluid, inimitable needs of your organization and community, including current and future risks, better than you. Thus, I encourage you to be creative and have fun with it. However, I caution you to ensure that your chosen format and implementation meets or exceeds accreditation standards, where applicable, state regulatory standards, such as POST, when required, and is completely congruent with any union contracts. Lastly, I encourage you to include all law enforcement personnel in the learning. While all education and training topics devised for sworn supervisory and sworn personnel may not be germane to telecommunications professionals, records clerks or secretaries, including civilian support personnel, to the fullest extent practicable has several advantages: it may improve their morale, efficiency, and job performance; it allows different personnel an accurate frame of reference for each other's interfacing roles; it reinforces organizational values and identity; it encourages creativity and promotes the free exchange of ideas; and it creates the synergy necessary for developing learning and accountability partnerships. Universally relevant topics include:

- all facets of *leadership*—community stakeholders rightfully expect all police personnel to effectively lead and any employee could potentially be the face or voice of any law enforcement learning organization;

- *community-oriented policing and problem-solving*—because this is an organization-wide philosophy requiring commitment from all personnel;
- *employee wellness*—an inherent human need;
- *communication and soft skills*—the foundation of human connection and the best defense against liability;
- *developing emotional and social intelligence*—this is critical for transformational leadership and crisis management;
- *cultural adroitness*—because our organizations and communities are becoming increasingly diverse;
- *sexual harassment awareness and prevention*—consider the #MeToo movement decimating Hollywood and American politics;
- *civil rights awareness*—necessary for values-driven, fair law enforcement, and customer service;
- *disability awareness*—directly related to civil rights and civil liberties;
- *crisis intervention*—another potential source of liability;
- *addictions*—the significance of the national opioid epidemic cannot be overstated;
- *police and emotionally disturbed persons*—this population is extremely likely to regularly interact with law enforcement personnel;
- *suicide prevention*—preservation of human life is a traditional core value of law enforcement learning organizations and can be especially challenging in organizations operating a jail;
- *police and elderly persons*—this vulnerable population is rapidly increasing and often dependent on law enforcement services;
- *terrorism awareness*—prevention is a shared responsibility;
- and a host of other organization-specific and community-specific topics.

Larger organizations with personnel dedicated exclusively to developing and implementing education and training may be able to centralize this endeavor. Smaller organizations depending more on cross-functionality, may choose to delegate such responsibilities to one or a few qualified personnel in addition to their other duties.

I urge you to contact your respective state's law enforcement regulatory body for guidance, including specific education and certification in this area. For example, in New York, the Division of Criminal Justice Services offers a two-week Instructor Development Course. This challenging, topical course equips law enforcement personnel with the knowledge and skills to research, develop, and deliver education and training courses within their organizations and communities. In these type of courses, topics typically include, but may not limited to: *devising education and training needs; curricula development; principles of adult learning; formulating instructional/learning objectives; crafting lesson plans; effectively using audiovisual aids; developing exams and other comprehension checks; public speaking; and legal aspects and obligations of recordkeeping.*

These types of comprehensive instructor-preparation courses mandate law enforcement practitioners' research and develop an entire class in a topic outside of their respective areas of expertise. Then, they teach the class before their fellow aspiring instructors, under the tutelage of state-certified, senior- or master-level police instructors. Of course, students receive continual feedback and encouragement. Ultimately, they must meet or exceed several challenging benchmarks before being certified as General Topics Instructors.

Once state-certified police instructor status is attained, practitioners may have opportunities to earn train-the-trainer instructor certifications. These specialty instructor certifications include: firearms; defensive tactics; mental health; suicide prevention; emergency vehicle operation; and a host of others. Master Instructor certification may also be available. These advanced-level instructor certification courses are designed to equip law enforcement practitioners to certify and oversee entry-level instructors and entire police education and training divisions or law enforcement academies.

Obviously, unless the law enforcement practitioners developing in-service education and training are competent and credible in doing so, the actual education and training likely won't meet even minimum standards and acceptable practices. In fact, as discussed in chapter 3, when facing expert legal scrutiny, it is very likely to eventually be found deficient or even negligent. Moreover, as noted in chapter 4, law enforcement accreditation standards are stringent. These standards always require a written course announcement; course registration and attendance records; justification of instructor competence or expertise; a formal lesson plan, including source citations; clearly-defined learning objectives; and a measurable comprehension check. Further, most states regulate law enforcement education and training records under statutory education law or as business records. Of course, as referenced in chapter 1, all potential civil litigation against law enforcement organizations will eventually require releasing all requested records. Therefore, the importance of meticulously organizing and maintaining both electronic and hard copies of these records cannot be overstated.

What if your state or province doesn't have a law enforcement instructor certification course? In that case, I urge you to partner with professional educators in colleges or universities. Often, professors of criminal justice are willing to teach law enforcement practitioners education-based skills similar to what they would learn in a police instructor certification course. These are outstanding opportunities for mutually advantageous partnerships. Police personnel can reciprocate by being guest lecturers in college or university classes and by participating in college and career initiatives. Moreover, law enforcement learning organizations can offer students semester-long internships. With the recruiting and retention challenges facing many law enforcement organizations, this may be the most reliable, low-cost recruiting strategy. I was employed by a law enforcement organization in Upstate New York that had such a partnership. At one point, 64% of the organization's sworn personnel had completed the internship program before graduating from a community college. In the interest of full disclosure and complete transparency, I was also a member of that college's adjunct faculty. One of my faculty duties was coordinating the criminal justice internship program. Thus, I urged the best students to request their internships with my law enforcement organization. This afforded ten weeks to determine if they'd like to have a career there while providing the organization an opportunity to convince student-interns that it was a desirable workplace. Further, it afforded the organization a valid, adequate sample of the student-interns' behavior, character, and performance. I viewed it as a developmental opportunity, similar to the practice squad of players every NFL team maintains.

As noted in chapter 4, I designed the Values-Oriented, Daily Ten-Minute Education and Training Model to augment twenty-one hours of annual, accreditation-driven in-service education and training. Since that organization in Upstate New York held in-service education fifteen days annually and firearms training fifteen days annually, all sworn personnel completed a total of twenty-one hours of education. This was done in 3, seven-hour increments; supplemented by 3, two-hour firearms training sessions, totaling twenty-seven hours of in-service education and training. Since police personnel typically worked 214 days annually, that left 208 working days without education and training. This was a tremendous missed opportunity. Therefore, if police personnel had been educated in accordance with the Values-Oriented, Ten-Minute Daily Education and Training Model, they would have completed an additional thirty-four hours of cost-free annual in-service education.

The first organization I was privileged to lead as chief of police was also in Upstate New York. Thus, the shift structure, including paid, fifteen-minute pre-shift briefing time, staggering of regular days off, and state accreditation mandates mirrored the organization where, ten years earlier, I'd implemented the Values-Oriented, Ten-minute Daily Education and Training Model pilot program. Hence, logistically, the implementation challenges were negligible.

Before offering step-by-step recommendations for formatting and implementing the Values-Oriented, Ten-Minute Daily Education and Training Model, I'd like to briefly review the broad tenets necessary for transforming a traditional law enforcement organization into a law enforcement learning organization: The blueprint for orchestrating and sustaining organizational change, including gaining all-important commitment, as articulated in chapter 1; the necessity of a singular organizational identity based on shared core values, as described in chapter 2; the importance of risk identification, strategic management, and strategic objectives and goals, as delineated in chapter 3; and the critical role of organizational policy, as outlined in Chapter Four. I urge you to frequently refer to the key points in those chapters during every stage of your organizational transformation; and while formatting and implementing the Values-Oriented, Ten-Minute Daily Education and Training Model.

It's important to note that the best practice awarded the Values-Oriented, Ten-Minute Daily Education and Training Model considered four key points: *the self-study concept of formal daily education, the emphasis on organizational values, the all-inclusive, standardized modular format, and the comprehension check fostering learning and accountability partnerships between supervisory personnel and their respective direct reports*. Thus, while the model is portable, conducive to modification, and perhaps even improvement, I'll share the award-winning methodology of implementing and formatting.

Modular education and training consists of standardized units. Typically, designing law enforcement in-service education modules entails identifying specific educational needs, formulating clearly-defined learning or instructional objectives, identifying the standard content elements, incorporating a measurable comprehension check, and creating a template for reuse. Therefore, I offer the following seven-step guide for transforming the Values-Oriented, Ten-Minute Daily Education and Training Model from abstract concept to best practice reality:

1. Establish and implement a formal policy identifying the Values-Oriented, Ten-Minute Daily Education and Training Model as an integral part of the law enforcement learning organization's fabric, clearly outlining the processes for development, implementation, completion, quality control, and assessment.

2. In accordance with accreditation mandates, if applicable, and for logistical practicality, disseminate an organization-wide course announcement for each Values-Oriented, Ten-Minute Daily Education module course.

3. Design and implement the modular or other desired format, including provisions for a formal lesson plan.

4. Select and implement a vessel for accessing and delivering the Values-Oriented, Ten-Minute courses, such as the organizational Intranet, in concert with Microsoft PowerPoint, via desktop or laptop computer. Your learning organization's Information Technology specialists should have significant input into how rudimentary or sophisticated these processes are. Of course, availability of organizational resources will also factor into this decision.

5. Select a comprehension check, such as verbal, in conjunction with a supervisory inquiry; or written, in the form of a multiple-choice examination.

6. Choose a method commensurate with established organizational protocol for recordkeeping, storage and retrieval; electronic or hard copy; or both.

7. In order to ensure the effectiveness of the Values-Oriented, Ten-Minute Education and Training Model, assessment must occur. The assessment process will be discussed in chapter 6.

Each of these seven-steps will be described in greater depth as follows:

Step 1. Assuming you've already taken the inaugural communication-based actions described in chapter 1 and gained the necessary commitment or buy-in from key personnel, a **formal policy** is essential. The policy can be all-inclusive: the commitment to a law enforcement learning organization; explaining the in-service education and training format; and articulating the role and structure of the Values-Oriented, Ten-Minute Education and Training Model; or three separate, sequential policies. This is truly a matter of personal preference. However, accrediting bodies often have mandates based on standards or preferences designed to make the assessment team's multi-day assessment easier and more efficient. Therefore, if your law enforcement learning organization is accredited, or striving toward accreditation, the accreditation manager/team should have input into this decision. As a former organizational accreditation manager and certified state-wide assessor, I discourage you from titling and numbering organizational policies in alignment with accreditation standards. While logical, and well-intentioned, this creates angst for accreditation teams. This is because most accredited organizations have more policies than accreditation standards. Hence, this can create confusion for assessors.

The policy should include a mechanism for directing the format and implementation; and controlling the process governing completion and supervision of the Values-Oriented, Ten-Minute Daily Education and Training Model.

Step 2. Every four-part module course requires an organization-wide **course announcement**. The course announcement should outline procedures for completing and documenting completion of the daily modules, deadlines for completion, and a method for supervisory affirmation and documentation that all applicable personnel met the comprehension check of all learning objectives. This should be in a standardized template capable of reuse. Consider the following example:

Anywhere Police Department
Education and Professional Development Division
COURSE ANNOUNCEMENT

To: All Commands
From: Captain Hogan Dalton, Director of Education and Professional Development
Date: 02/12/2018
Subject: Ten-Minute Daily Education; Session Two; Section Three; Modules I – IV
Cc: A.C. Wilhelm, Chief of Police
Purnell J. Rigsby, Deputy Chief of Police

Please be advised that in accordance with General Order O-212-1, 'Risk Management: Values-Oriented, Ten-Minute Daily In-service

Education and Training,' Session Two, Section Three, Modules I – IV of the Anywhere Police Department's 2018 Values-Oriented, Ten-Minute Daily Education and Training will begin on Monday 02/19/2018. These modules comprise the following topics: Module I; 'Overview of Sexual Harassment Awareness and Prevention;' Module II; 'Quid-pro-quo Sexual Harassment Awareness and Prevention;' Module III; 'Hostile Workplace Environment Awareness and Prevention;' and Module IV; 'Third-Party and Same-Sex Harassment, Reporting Procedures, and Supervisory Responsibilities.'

Satisfactory completion of this four-module course addressing sexual harassment in the workplace is **<u>mandatory</u> for all sworn-supervisory, sworn, and civilian personnel.** All personnel will complete each daily module during their paid, fifteen-minute pre-shift briefing period.

In order to access the modules, all personnel will register through the APD's Intranet, using their individual organizational e-mail account and password. Upon individual completion of each module and following supervisory affirmation that all four learning objectives were met, approving supervisors will ensure that individual personnel affix their electronic signature on the roster in the area designated 'learning objectives met.' Affirming supervisors will also affix their electronic signature on the roster in the area designated 'supervisory affirmation.' Affirming supervisors will then print and sign the hard copy of the roster.

All 'designated' Shift and Division supervisors will, daily, place all completed and affirmed electronic versions of rosters in an electronic folder, and e-mail the respective folders to Sergeant L.T. Boomer, at the following e-mail address: sergeantboomer@anywherepd.org Further, all designated supervisors will, daily, place all hard copies of completed and affirmed rosters in an inter-office envelope and place all envelopes and contents in the Education and Professional Development Division's depository, located outside of room 222. The depository is under recorded video surveillance and will serve as an additional record of compliance. The transfer of all completed and affirmed electronic and hard copy rosters to the Education and Professional Development Division will be completed no later than the conclusion of each 'designated' Shift and Division supervisor's daily tour-of-duty.

Ten-Minute Daily Education Session Two, Section Three will conclude with the completion of Module IV on 02/22/2018.

The Education and Professional Development Division will audit compliance. Shift and Division commanders will be notified of any non-compliance, including personnel absent with authorization. If necessary, make-up dates and times will be scheduled at a time of mutual convenience.

Any inquiries should be directed to the Director of Education and Professional Development, at extension # 4551 or at the following e-mail address: captaindalton@anywherepd. org Thank you, in advance, for your cooperation.

Sincerely,
Captain Hogan Dalton
Captain Hogan Dalton, MPA
Graduate, FBI National Academy, 216th Session
Graduate, FBI-LEEDA Trilogy, 2015

Step 3. Designing and implementing the **modular format** is less labor-intensive and more convenient for law enforcement education/training practitioners than other formats. The sequential structure of the modular format is well-suited to adult learning. This is because it begins with known material and transitions to the unknown; starts with simple concepts and flows into more complex matters; and begins with easier notions that segue into more challenging ideas. Further, the modular format is portable. In other words, it can be easily modified to the specific needs of every law enforcement learning organization.

I used four, ten-minute modules per course. Each ten-minute module comprised the following characteristics: four instructional objectives, the first of which was directly correlated to integrating the organizational values; [start with *Why*] a verbal comprehension check verified and documented by a supervisory officer; the organizational *Why* statement; and a lesson plan, including source citations.

Each module contained an excerpt from an organizational policy germane to the related topics addressed in the modules. For example, Module I: 'Sexual Harassment Awareness and Prevention,' General Order O-214-1, 'Prohibition of Sexual Harassment and Hostile Workplace Environment.' The policy excerpt should define sexual harassment and describe organizational education-based and supervisory efforts toward prevention.

Module II: 'Quid-pro-quo Sexual Harassment Awareness and Prevention, General Order O-214-1-A., 'Prohibition of Quid-Pro-Quo Sexual Harassment.' The policy excerpt should define quid-pro-quo or something-for-something harassment and provide some common examples.

Module III: 'Hostile Workplace Environment Awareness and Prevention,' General Order O-214-1-B., 'Prohibition of Sexual Harassment and Hostile Workplace Environment.' The policy excerpt should define hostile environment harassment and provide some common examples.

Module IV: 'Third-Party and Same-Sex Harassment,' General Order O-214-1-C., 'Prohibition of Sexual Harassment and Hostile

Workplace Environment.' The policy excerpt should define third-party and same-sex harassment, provide some common examples, identify reporting obligations and procedures, supervisory mandates, and potential redress of offenders.

Step 4. My preferred format for **accessing the modules** was the law enforcement learning organization's **Intranet**. This restricted communications network using World Wide Web software offered a cost-effective, efficient means of accessing, navigating, and storing vast amounts of education-based data. The **modules** were **delivered** through **Microsoft PowerPoint, via desktop or laptop computer.** This format has several advantages: ease in development, including all-inclusive learning objectives, lesson plan, and video embedding; ease of adding color, visual transitions, audio transitions, graphics, and links to policies or websites; ease of modification to accommodate organizational personnel with learning disabilities, in accordance with the reasonable accommodation provision of the Americans with Disabilities Act; ease of navigation by police personnel; ease of supervisory affirmation of the comprehension check; and ease of electronic and traditional hard copy recordkeeping and retrieval.

Each module typically comprised eight to ten slides, including a cover slide and lesson plan. Consider the following example:

Slide 1

The first slide is a cover slide with the module number and title, and organizational logo and colors.

Anywhere Police Department

Risk Management: Values-Oriented, Ten-Minute Daily Education Module I; 'Sexual Harassment Awareness and Prevention'

ORGANIZATIONAL LOGO

Slide 2

Since these are values-based education modules, the second slide contains a truncated version of the organizational values statement.

CORE VALUES
United in cause, purpose, and belief we, the dedicated professionals of the Anywhere Police Department, embrace, and live by the following core values:

HUMAN LIFE
We value human life and dignity as guaranteed by the U.S. Constitution.

INTEGRITY
We believe that integrity is the basis for constituent trust.

LAWS and CONSTITUTION
We support the principles embodied in the U.S. Constitution.

EXCELLENCE
We relentlessly strive for personal and professional excellence.

ACCOUNTABILITY
We are personally accountable to each other and the stakeholders we serve.

COMMUNITY PARTNERSHIP
We are committed to community policing as a philosophy, not merely a program or initiative.

Slide 3

The third slide contains the organizational *Why* Statement.

OUR WHY

United in a spirit of teamwork, driven by a resolute commitment to our shared values, the dedicated professionals of the Anywhere Police Department recognize that every sustainable relationship arises from a personal, human need. Police personnel strive to connect to stakeholders' intellectual and emotional needs, form partnerships, and create empowerment opportunities for unprecedented community safety and quality-of-life. Unyielding in this purpose, and dedicated to live by our principles, we are devoted to ensuring a paradigm-breaking customer experience, while making a positive difference toward the greater cause of the State of Anywhere.

Slide 4

The fourth slide of each module contains the four learning objectives.

- At the conclusion of this Values-Oriented, Daily Ten-Minute self-study in-service education module, each sworn-supervisory, sworn, and civilian learning and accountability partner will, with or without referencing the provided slide show and policy excerpt, correctly verbally answer supervisory inquiries or questions, concerning the following four learning objectives:

  1. Which of our organizational core values can you inter-link with the topic of sexual harassment awareness and prevention?
  2. Define sexual harassment, in accordance with the definition provided by Human Resource Magazine and affirmed by organizational General Order O-214-1, 'Prohibition of Sexual Harassment and Hostile Workplace Environment.'
  3. The nexus between acts of sexual harassment and possible allegations of civil rights violations.

4. Four approaches all organizational personnel should prac-
    tice to prevent sexual harassment from occurring in the
    workplace.

Slide 5

- According to HR Magazine, and affirmed by organizational G.O. O-214-1, sexual harassment is any unwanted tacit, verbal or physical conduct of a sexual nature. It includes, but is not limited to: inappropriate comments, gestures, e-mails, text messages, instant messages, jokes, photographs, props, videos, touching, and demands or requests for sexual favors as conditions of employment.
- Sexual harassment allegations have recently been on the rise across America. Hollywood mogul Harvey Weinstein, actor Kevin Spacey, talk show host Bill O'Reilly, and the NFL Network's Marshall Falk are a few of the well-known people recently accused of sexual harassment in the workplace.
- In law enforcement, the Algood, Tennessee PD and the El Cajon, California PD recently experienced well-publicized civil litigation based on complaints of sexual harassment in the workplace.

Slide 6

- The Anywhere Police Department's core values of human life, integrity, laws and constitution, excellence, accountability, and community partnership are incongruent with the odious nature and harmful outcomes associated with sexual harassment.
- The Anywhere Police Department has a zero-tolerance approach to all forms of sexual and workplace harassment, including retaliation. This is delineated in G.O. O-214-1, which states, "The Anywhere Police Department, in accordance with its core values and *Why*, is resolutely committed to preventing all forms of sexual and workplace harassment; and to providing a safe, inclusive, respectful environment for all sworn and civilian personnel, outside law enforcement personnel, and all other agents, contractors, and visitors. Further, the Anywhere Police Department will

not tolerate any form of retaliation for reporting any allegation of sexual or workplace harassment; or for cooperating in any related investigation."

Slide 7

- Since sexual harassment is a form of discrimination, persistent and pervasive acts may rise to the level of civil rights violations.
- However, as a predictable risk, sexual and workplace harassment is preventable.
- All APD personnel must consider themselves risk managers, ready, willing, and able to detect and prevent sexual harassment; or report acts of sexual harassment; and take the necessary action in accordance with organizational policy and their respective job responsibilities.

Slide 8

- All APD personnel can prevent acts of sexual and workplace harassment by:
- Embracing and modeling our organizational core values and *Why*.
- Understanding and adhering to organizational policy.
- Modeling the learning that occurs through in-service education and training.
- Cultivating accountability partnerships between sworn-supervisory, sworn, and civilian personnel.
- Think **PETS**: **P**olicy; **E**ducation; **T**raining; **S**upervision.
- Policy Link: General Order General Order O-214-1, 'Prohibition of Sexual Harassment and Hostile Workplace Environment.

Slide 9

LESSON PLAN – 1 of 2

Course: Risk Management; Ten-Minute Daily Education; Session Two; Section Three; Module I.

Lesson Title: 'Sexual Harassment Awareness and Prevention in the
Workplace.'
Dates: 02/19 – 02/22/2018
Time / Duration: 10 Minutes.
Method: Self-Study; Module-Based; Power Point Slide Show Format.
Location: Anywhere Police Department.
Prerequisites: Sworn-Supervisory, Sworn or Civilian Member of the
APD.
Pre-test: None Post-test: None. Objectives: [4] See Slide 4.
Comprehension Check: Oral; Supervisory Inquiry.
Prepared By: Captain Hogan Dalton, State-Certified MA/GT/IE/
MH/CT.
Approved By: Deputy Chief Purnell J. Rigsby, State-Certified MA/GT.

Slide 10

LESSON PLAN – 2 of 2

Preparer's References: [4]

1. NBC TV: Dateline; **The Sex Wars**, 60 Minute Documentary,
    Phillips, Reynolds, October – 1997, [Referenced, Not Viewed
    by Learning Partners.]
2. HR Magazine: **Sexual Harassment**; Editorial Excerpt, Coy,
    Cynthia, C., September – 2015.
3. APD Operation's Manual: **G.O. O-214-1**; Melton-Barnes,
    Lincoln, December – 2017.
4. APD Supervisory Training Bulletins: **Sexual Harassment
    Prevention,** Dalton, Hogan, December – 2007 – 2017 – Revised
    or Attested Annually.

Learning Partners' Aids: Desktop/Laptop Computer, PP Slide Show
Containing 10 Slides, Organizational Intranet, Individual
E-mail Accounts for Registration and Completion.
Records Storage: Electronic and Hard Copies.
Accreditation Compliant: Yes.

The remaining three modules of every course would follow the same format and look very similar to the above example. This course should segue into the next four-module course. For example, since sexual harassment is a form of discrimination, 'Civil Rights Awareness,' as described in chapter 3, would be logical as the next four-module course.

Step 5. As noted in slide nine, my **preferred comprehension check was oral, verified by supervisory inquiry**. This entailed supervisory personnel being conspicuous while their direct reports were completing the Values-Oriented, Ten-Minute Daily modules. Upon completion of each module, non-supervisory and supervisory personnel formed an intellectual and emotional connection over a conversation about the contents of the module. Non-supervisory employees verbalized the correct answers to all four objectives. Supervisory personnel, in accordance with the protocol delineated in the general order, and reiterated in the Course Announcement memorandum, verified that the benchmark was achieved. Supervisors then carried-out the process of documentation as spelled out in the general order and reiterated in the Course Announcement memorandum.

The same procedure occurred organization-wide. Captains partnering with and verifying that lieutenants had met the learning objectives; lieutenants partnering with and verifying that sergeants had met the learning objectives, etc.

The great Gordon Graham espoused the value of cops demonstrating knowledge-based proficiency by passing written exams. It's a valid argument. It's also easy enough to accomplish. It simply entails a partnership between those developing the daily modules and Information Technology personnel creating a matrix on the law enforcement learning organization's Intranet. Again, the portability of the model is part of its allure. I preferred the oral/supervisory verification approach because it developed learning and accountability partnerships between supervisory and non-supervisory personnel and among first-line and second-line supervisors, all the way up through the organizational hierarchy. The learning and accountability partnership aspect was very meaningful to the NASPA board when awarding the Values-Oriented, Ten-Minute Daily Education and Training Model an industry-wide best practice.

Learning and accountability partnership is not a platitude. It's truly at the heart of every law enforcement learning organization's core values and *Why*. You may recall that in chapter 2 I postulated that the CEO and all executive-level, command-level, and supervisory-level law enforcement leaders must become accountability stewards as "chief accountability partners of values." Additionally, I opined that core values are also a guiding force in retiring or removing those personnel who are unwilling or unable to live, breathe, and bleed them.

During my second tenure as a police chief, I attempted to establish a personal, one-on-one learning and accountability partnership with a command-level disagreeable whom I referenced in chapter 2. This individual insisted that, along with all other organizational personnel and in accordance with established policy and procedure, he had been navigating the module-based slide shows. However, he consistently failed to meet the comprehension check under the oral/supervisory verification approach. This became a great source of consternation for him, as he was forced to continually repeat Module I. A control mechanism built into the system revealed that he had been navigating each module for about 45 seconds. Thus, while a learning partnership was never properly established, the individual was held strictly accountable for his leadership failure and refusal to model our organizational *why* and core values.

Step 6. Every member of every law enforcement learning organization has heard and said it countless times, "If it wasn't documented, it never happened." That axiom is often invoked in the context of a supervisory officer correcting the inappropriate actions of a follower but failing to commit to writing what occurred, how it was addressed, and future expectations. Thus, failure to document in that context, removes progressive discipline from any similar future inappropriate actions by the same follower.

Following that same logic, *every law enforcement learning organization's education and training is only as exemplary as its recordkeeping, storage, and retrieval.* Thus, I recommend selecting and implementing a method commensurate with established best practices, encompassing electronic storage and back-up, and hard copy storage. The hard copy storage should be secure, as such records often contain personal or sensitive information of law enforcement personnel. Further, hard copy storage should be impervious to theft, tampering, and damage from fire, water, and rodents.

While codirector of a regional law enforcement academy on a college campus, we stored hard copy records inside of cardboard computer paper boxes in a loft between the inner roof and the administrative offices. Upon retrieving some records on behalf of one of the organizations served by that academy, some of the paper had been chewed by mice and sustained minor damage. Fortunately, it was not catastrophic. However, it was a lesson learned.

Several years later at the same academy, I wasn't that fortunate. While serving as codirector, I had the education and training records of my police organization assiduously organized and maintained. They were stored in locked filing cabinets, protected from all discernible threats. I'd also begun the process of computerizing all education and training records. Upon being promoted and in accordance with contractual agreement, I was transferred from the academy to police headquarters. Several years, and three academy codirectors later, the academy relocated from a public college to a private university. Ostensibly, during the move, an entire filing cabinet and contents were misplaced – and never recovered. Moreover, electronic replication of the files had never been completed. Another lesson learned. This time, a painful, embarrassing one.

Step 7. Assessment is the final of the seven recommended steps for implementing and formatting the Values-Oriented, Ten-Minute Daily Education and Training Model. Assessing the effectiveness of this component of a law enforcement learning organization will be discussed at length in chapter 6.

As *your* learning and accountability partner, I recognize that these are volatile, uncertain times for America's finest. Thus, I'm driven to do anything I can to improve the wellness, vitality, personal safety, reputation, and longevity of all law enforcement personnel. By establishing law enforcement learning organizations and committing to daily education and edification, law enforcement leaders never settle for the conventional. On behalf of their followers and organizations, they purposefully reinvent, and boldly depart from the status quo. I hope you'll agree, this is no longer merely a recommended course of action, it's truly the only reasonable course of action.

Chapter 5 Connection Questions

1. Why would you advocate for or against a verbal comprehension check in your law enforcement learning organization's Values-Oriented, Ten-Minute Daily Education modules?
2. What challenges, if any, do you anticipate with the integration of sworn and civilian/support personnel as learning and accountability partners?
3. How would you make the Values-Oriented, Ten-Minute Daily Education modules compliant with any requests from law enforcement learning organizational personnel for reasonable accommodation under the Americans with Disabilities Act?

Assessing the Values-Oriented, Daily Ten-Minute Education and Training Model

The greatest enemy of tomorrow's success is yesterday's success.

—Rick Warren

Transforming a traditional law enforcement organization into a law enforcement learning organization is the ultimate continuous process improvement initiative. Since strategic management, as explained in chapter 3, is designed to improve systems and processes, it's ideally suited to seminally analyze the current state of traditional operations and compare that picture to what best practices in a law enforcement learning organization look like. The SWOT component, as delineated on page 49, plays a critical role in developing a valid, consistent, reliable, continually-evolving assessment process. Thus, after piloting the Values-Oriented, Ten-Minute Daily Education and Training Model for 90–120 days, sufficient data will exist to accurately assess the effectiveness of the daily education, corresponding learning, and personal and organizational improvement. The duration of the assessment typically averages ten business days. Larger organizations, following the line-and-staff structure, may choose to allocate fifteen to twenty business days. Irrespective of the organizational variables, I offer the following eight steps to achieving a transparent assessment leading to continued best practices.

1. **Predetermine objectives, scope, and goal.** Law enforcement learning organizations must be clear about why assessment is being undertaken and the goal for how the results will be utilized. Clearly defining this will help determine the desired scope of the assessment and the selection of those who will complete the assessment. It's important to not only benchmark historically using performance assessment reports, personnel complaints and corresponding dispositions, early warning system activations, citizen satisfaction surveys, civil lawsuits, personnel satisfaction surveys, formal personal improvement plans, unfair labor practices, labor-related grievances, and other metrics, assessment must be forward-looking. Hence, law enforcement learning organizations must benchmark against the future potential of their teams and organizations. Therefore, strategic generational planning, including SMART goals, as described in chapter 3 is collectively oriented toward improvement. Thus, while success asks the question, "what is the organization getting?" Improvement always asks, "what is the organization becoming?"

Traditional law enforcement or law enforcement learning organizations that have earned either CALEA or any state-driven accreditation status, as described in chapter 4, will have undergone at least one comprehensive assessment across the operational spectrum. Thus, these organizations will have some familiarity and level of comfort with the assessment process. Further, preceding the assessment process, these organizations will also have participated in a pre-assessment. In colloquial terms, this is sometimes referred to as a "mock" assessment. The accreditation pre-assessment is designed to prepare the organization to pass the scrutiny of the actual assessment. However, unlike accreditation assessment, the previously described organization-wide SWOT analysis dispenses with the need for a formal pre-assessment of the Ten-Minute, Values-Oriented Daily Education and Training Model.

2. **Identify who will perform the assessment and how results will be delivered and shared**. Evaluate who would be the best law enforcement personnel and outside partners to conduct the assessment based on their knowledge and experience and how their capabilities align with the established objectives. Certified accreditation assessors may be ideal partners because of their background in law enforcement, research, and their experience in establishing incremental and breakthrough improvement. If using other partners from outside the law enforcement learning organization, research must be done and referrals obtained from professional contacts. Developing a list of questions to be used to evaluate your prospective partners is highly recommended. Academic practitioners from institutions of higher-learning, as discussed in chapter 5, may be suitable partners. This is because assessment is as natural as breathing in higher-learning institutions. Therefore, these partners lend tremendous expertise and credibility to the process. Lastly, think ahead to how results will be delivered and shared to make sure that the assessment results will have the desired impact on your law enforcement learning organization's future planning.

3. **Prepare the law enforcement learning organization for the assessment.** The quality of the assessment will depend on both who does the assessment and the people providing the information. All organizational personnel must be prepared to cooperate fully and willingly. Having a healthy singular organizational identity and *why*, as discussed in chapter 2, will be advantageous in this endeavor. However, any high-ranking disagreeables or rejecters, as defined in chapter 1, may overtly or through passive-aggressive behaviors sabotage the process. Hence, at least one member of the internal assessment team should have formal authority at least equal to the highest-ranking member of the organization from whom cooperation is sought. While explaining the purpose of the assessment and how the results will

be used is essential, law enforcement personnel will also want to know who will conduct the assessment and how the results will be compiled. Thus, assessment partners should be able to help prepare the organization with realistic expectations. Awareness sessions that describe industry benchmarks and best practices are a good way of creating awareness of the assessment purpose and increasing the desire for change. This also lessens the fears and promotes open dialogue about the current state.

4. **Orient the assessment team to the organizational *why* and to the work environment.** If using an external partner, in addition to understanding the organization's purpose, cause, and belief, they will also need to know what the organization does. Hence, they will need a lot of background information to prepare for the assessment. Promptly providing the requested information will help the assessment go smoothly. Make sure that the team knows everything they need to know about the work environment and plan for sworn supervisory, sworn, and civilian law enforcement personnel to be available when necessary for meetings and appointments. Once again, law enforcement learning organizations with established police/community relationships and partnerships will minimize the awkward getting-to-know-each-other period and have a more seamless process.

5. **Conduct the assessment using best practices to facilitate honest feedback and minimize resistance.** Stay in contact with assessment partners throughout the assessment period to make sure that they are collecting the feedback they need. Address any issues immediately since there is a short window for the information-gathering stage of an assessment. Manage any concerns or misperceptions among police personnel about the assessment process and objectives.

6. **Develop an action plan.** Simply reporting the results may be useful but developing an action plan using the [SMART] paradigm discussed in chapter 3: Specific, Measurable,

Actionable, Realistic, and Timely objectives shows exactly how the investment in the assessment and associated improvements will provide a return. The plan should take into account the investments in time, money, and resources that will be required to close any gaps and realize the collective benefits identified in the assessment. Hard questions should be asked. Hard truths, responded to openly, are a catalyst for improvement. For example, data may indicate that some underrepresented community members perceive patrol officers' behavior as procedurally unjust or some senior citizens view the SWAT team as over utilized and too militaristic. These concerns can be addressed in manifold ways. Education and training, of course, should play a key role.

7. **Communicate the results and the action plan.** Review with your partners the results of the assessment and how the results will be communicated to your leadership team. If there will be a formal presentation of the assessment results and business case or justification for amending or adjusting the Values-Oriented, Ten-Minute Daily Education Model, plan far enough ahead for the meeting so that the appropriate people will commit to attending and include the meeting in their schedules. Further, consider inviting key external partners, such as elected officials, community activists, business owners, members of the faith-based community, and the media. Getting commitment to the assessment results and business case is essential to being able to implement the actions that will improve performance.

8. **Implement the recommended actions.** The return on investment of the time and totality of resources invested in the assessment is in taking the actions recommended in the assessment results. This requires courageous leadership. Challenges must be anticipated and expected. Progress should be evaluated daily. Positive results and successes, both large and small, should be shared and celebrated. Continually recognizing individual personnel for their contributions validates the transformational change.

Failure is the other F word. It's the one that senior leaders in both traditional and law enforcement learning organizations often fear. Failure, however, can be a meaningful step in the sequence of success. I've had the distinct honor and high privilege of holding numerous supervisory, command, and executive positions in both traditional and law enforcement learning organizations. Therefore, I've experienced my share of failure. Fortunately, after my first failure, I realized that the sun would rise again. I've seen other leaders paralyzed by fear of failure. Many of these leaders allowed their fear of failure to control their attitudes and actions. Thus, they never led their followers and organizations to self-actualization or fulfillment of individual and organizational potential.

Factually, all real change, including transforming a traditional law enforcement organization into a law enforcement learning organization involves failure but not in the traditional sense. Remember, by definition, trial and error includes error. The key is developing the emotional intelligence and maturity to learn from failure and the resolve to try again. You may recall from chapter 4 that my first attempt to implement the Values-Oriented, Ten-Minute Daily Education and Training Model beyond the pilot stage failed. You may also recall that I viewed that failure as an opportunity for learning and personal growth. Eventually, the model was recognized as a best practice.

I feel like these pages have been a mutual learning and accountability journey. Therefore, as learning and accountability partners, I'd like to leave you with a few final thoughts. Personal growth and organizational improvement doesn't occur by happenstance. It's strategic and intentional. I urge you to invest in yourself by making daily learning and growth a top priority by recognizing and diligently seeking learning opportunities in every interaction and situation.

Lastly, you may recall in chapter 4 that I alluded to moments in life when vision, steadfast commitment, and partnering pay off. For writers that moment comes when they type "The End." Although this is the conclusion of the first of what I hope will be many books I write, I'm not going to write "The End" because this is just the beginning of a vast, new learning adventure. My hope is that your commitment to daily learning and improvement transcends law enforcement and becomes your lifestyle. Once you experience the dynamic, impactful change, you'll never be satisfied with anything less.

Chapter 6 Connection Questions

1. Why do you believe external partners should or should not be included in the assessment process?
2. What strategies would you use while advocating for or against configuring the post-assessment action plan in accordance with the SMART paradigm?
3. How have you transformed any personal or professional failures into successes?

Afterword

This book, like most books addressing police operations, contains a plethora of information. Since the Values-Oriented, Ten-Minute Daily Education and Training Model is designed to be portable, I'm hopeful that law enforcement professionals across the globe will be inspired to modify the matrix specific to their fluid organizational and community needs. I'm also optimistic that the concepts necessary for transformation to a law enforcement learning organization allow police leaders, educators, and trainers to use their creativity and leadership to achieve unprecedented success within their available organizational and community resources. Thus, I would like to reiterate the main theme of this book and what I hope it accomplishes for your personnel and individual law enforcement organizations.

I recommend that assessing education and training needs be a continuous, organization-wide process, emphasizing risk management. While liability is omnipresent in policing, identifiable or quantifiable risks can most often be avoided or at least mitigated. A main tenet of any sound risk management philosophy in policing emphasizes edification of police personnel by committing to best practices through daily education and training. Therefore, upper-level leaders and managers must be resolutely committed to developing and maintaining a learning organization where police personnel continually expand their capacity to create the results they truly desire, where new and expansive patterns of thinking are nurtured, where collective aspiration is set free, and where employees are continually learning how to learn together.

I encourage you to make the organizational *why* and core values conspicuous in every self-study module. Further, I urge you align organizational policies with current best practices and amalgamate one or two germane policy or general order references into every module.

I advocate for the intimate involvement of all supervisory police personnel. First-line supervisors play an especially critical role in the success of this endeavor particularly in maintaining standardization and uniformity and ensuring integrity of the process. Further, because of their importance in inspiring the organizational *why*, and the fact that every police department is only as effective as its least effective first-line supervisor, these supervisors should receive frequent professional development education and training beyond the Ten-Minute Daily dynamic. This education and training should focus on leadership development and continuously improving supervisory and management skills.

I urge you to also educate civilian and support personnel with this model. These important members of law enforcement organizations often feel underappreciated, even forgotten. Since all community constituents and stakeholders expect all law enforcement personnel to be leaders, this model provides a propitious opportunity to equip them with the essential knowledge and skills to effectively lead in their respective roles.

Lastly, I implore you to ensure that the commitment to continuous learning is enjoyable. When learning is fun, police personnel will never be satisfied with their base of knowledge. Thus, they will be eternally curious for new and better information. They will not only learn it, they'll live it, they'll impart it to others, and they'll be accountability partners for each other.

Bibliography

Books

Fyfe, James, J., Greene, Jack, R., McLaren, Roy, Clinton, Walsh, William, F., Wilson, O.W. *Police Administration Fifth Edition.* New York, NY USA: McGraw-Hill, 1997.

Gamble, John, Thompson, Jr., Arthur. *Essentials of Strategic Management Fifth Edition.* New York, NY USA: McGraw-Hill, 2017.

Goleman, Daniel. *On Emotional Intelligence.* Boston, Massachusetts USA: Harvard Business Review, 2015.

Luntz, Frank, I. *Win the Key Principles to Take Your Business from Ordinary to Extraordinary.* New York, NY USA: Hyperion, 2011.

Luntz, Frank, I. *Words That Work.* New York, NY, USA: Hyperion, 2007.

Maxwell, John, C. *Developing the Leader Within You 2.0.* Nashville, TN USA: Harper Collins Leadership, 2018.

Sinek, Simon. *Start with Why How Great Leaders Inspire Everyone to Take Action.* New York, NY USA: Penguin Group, 2009.

Walsh, J. Martyn, Walsh, Anna Kathleen. *Plain English Handbook.* New York, NY USA: Random House, 1982.

Periodicals

Basile, Chad, Joyner, Chuck. *The Dynamic Resistance Response Model: A Modern Approach to Use of Force.* Federal Bureau of Investigation, Quantico, VA USA: FBI L.E. Bulletin: September 2007 Edition.

Garvin, David, A. *Building a Learning Organization*. Boston, Massachusetts USA: Harvard Business Review, July-August 1993 Issue.

Police Organizational Directives

Annual Performance Assessment Report [Organization not Identified; See Disclaimer, Page 11].

Pre-Employment Polygraph Questionnaire [Organization not Identified; See Disclaimer, Page 11].

Professional Development Symposium Excerpts

Daigle, Eric. *Agency Liability: Effective and Constitutional Policing*. In partnership with the Daigle Law Group, Southington, CT. Presented at the New York State Association Chiefs of Police conference, at the High Peaks Resort, in Lake Placid, NY on 07/16/14.

Daigle, Eric. *Police Operations: Implications Post-DOJ Review of Ferguson*. In partnership with the Daigle Law Group, Southington, CT. Presented at the FBI-Law Enforcement Executive Development Association conference at the Memphis, TN Convention Center, on 04/26/2016.

Davis, Michael, Fridell, Lorie, McBride, Michael, McQuay, Katherine. *Is Your Sub-Conscious Interfering with Your Policing? A Primer on Developing a Fair, Impartial Police Department*. In partnership with the Brooklyn Park Police Department, the University of South Florida, the PICO Network, and the United States Department of Justice. Presented at the International Association Chiefs of Police convention, at the Philadelphia Convention Center, on 10/20/13.

Graham, Gordon. *Risk Management in Public Safety: Predictable is Preventable*. Presented at the Western New York Law Enforcement Symposium at Hilbert College, on 11/12/2003.

Graham, Gordon. *Public Safety Risk Awareness for Law Enforcement Executives*. Presented at the FBI National Academy Associates conference, at the Philadelphia Convention Center, on 07/22/2014.

Miller, Kimberly, A. *Transforming Organizational Culture*. In partnership with K.A. Miller & Associates, Fort Collins, CO. Presented at the FBI Law Enforcement Executive Development Association conference at the Memphis, TN Convention Center, on 04/26/2016.

Student Course Manuals

Whalen, David, V. *First Responders Disability Awareness Training Student Manual*. New York State Department of Mental Health, in partnership with Niagara University, 2013.

Websites

www.asecrelife.com
www.brainyquote.com
www.businessdictionary.com
www.calea.org/content/resources
www.caselaw4cops.net/useofforce
www.cops.usdoj.gov/pdf/taskforce/taskforcefinalreport.pdf
www.dictionary.com
www.findlaw.com/constitution
www.hbr.org/1993/07/building-a-learning-organization
www.iacp.org/policies
www.lexipol.com/tip-of-the-day/decisionmaking
www.simplypsychologytoday/com/maslowhierarchy
www.onesourcevirtual.com
www.sgr.com/10in10/values
www.vbgov.com/police
www.yourdictionary.com/riskmanagement
www.youtube.com/organizationalidentity

About the Author

Les Kachurek entered law enforcement at the age of twenty. During a career that spanned four decades, six police departments, and four states, he spent eighteen years in command and executive leadership positions. As chief of police, he led the transformation of two police departments to law enforcement learning organizations. He retired from policing in 2016 to pursue his passions of teaching and writing. Les joined the faculty of FBI-LEEDA in 2016 and has been traveling internationally, teaching best practices in leadership to law enforcement practitioners, human resource professionals, and legal advisers.

A lifelong learner, Les holds Bachelor of Science and Master of Science degrees in Criminal Justice from Southwest University in Kenner, Louisiana. He also holds Master of Business Administration and Master of Arts in Organizational Management degrees from Southwest University. Les is a graduate of the 216th Session of the FBI National Academy and the FBI Law Enforcement Executive Development Association's Leadership Trilogy. He holds a Graduate Certificate in Proactive Leadership from Cornell University, is certified by the Society for Human Resource Management as a Human Resource Professional, and the New York State Division of Criminal Justice Services as a Police Executive, Strategic Planner, and Master Police Instructor. He is a member of Southwest University's Honor Society and serves on Southwest University's Criminal Justice Advisory Board.

Regarded as a talented researcher, gifted writer, and dynamic public speaker, Les culled from his doctoral dissertation and presented at the FBI National Academy on behalf of the FBI's holistic wellness initiative, "Project Beyond Survival Toward Officer Wellness." He was also a panelist on the FBI Television Network's three-hour global broadcast, *The Spirit of the Law, Part II.*

Les has received numerous national, regional, and local awards, including Best Practices in Prevention, and Best Practices in General Campus Safety from Student Affairs Professionals in Higher Education 2014.